I 00

346

URBAN JUSTICE

URBAN JUSTICE
Law and Order
in
American Cities

HERBERT JACOB

Northwestern University

Generously Donated to
The Frederick Douglass Institute
By Professor Jesse Moore
Fall 2000

PRENTICE-HALL, INC., Englewood Cliffs, New Jersey

Library of Congress Cataloging in Publication Data

JACOB, HERBERT
    Urban justice.

    1. Municipal courts—United States.   2. Justice,
Administration of—United States.   3. Law and
politics.   I. Title.
KF8737.J3   347   73-399
ISBN 0-13-938951-2
ISBN 0-13-938944-X (pbk)

10 9 8 7 6 5 4

PRINTED IN THE UNITED STATES OF AMERICA

Prentice-Hall International, Inc., *London*
Prentice-Hall of Australia, Pty. Ltd., *Sydney*
Prentice-Hall of Canada, Ltd., *Toronto*
Prentice-Hall of India Private Limited, *New Delhi*
Prentice-Hall of Japan, Inc., *Tokyo*

For Joel, David, and Jenny

CONTENTS

PREFACE

This book is the product of a decade of research and teaching on problems of the administration of justice in America; at the same time, it is the prologue for a more intensive analysis of the criminal prosecution process in Chicago, Detroit, and Baltimore which I am just beginning with James Eisenstein. It is not an opening statement—as my book *Justice in America* was—but it certainly is not my final judgment about justice in American cities. Its conclusions may be too somber for some readers but they reflect my clearer perception of the problems plaguing the administration of justice than of their solutions.

I am heavily indebted to the many scholars whom I cite. Less evident but equally important is my debt to the students who have heard me expound and develop the views expressed in this book and who have subjected them to their critiques. I am especially grateful to three colleagues at Northwestern University who read all or much of the manuscript of this book and made many valuable suggestions: H. Paul Friesema, Louis H. Masotti, and Wesley G. Skogan. My other colleagues provided the kind of intellectual climate that even in difficult days have made the Northwestern Department of Political Science a good place in which to teach, research, and write. Of course, whatever errors of fact or judgment remain are entirely my own.

Evanston, Illinois   HERBERT JACOB

one

CITY POLITICS AND JUSTICE

City politics means conflict over housing, zoning, expressways and mass transit, schools, and even trash collection. It involves elected officials, city employees and their powerful unions, neighborhood groups, suppliers and ordinary voters. The city supplies a myriad of services for its inhabitants, who in turn compete with one another for advantageous treatment. The good schools, neat alleys, smooth streets, and convenient, clean parks that mark "desirable" neighborhoods are the booty of the winners; the dilapidated schools, garbage strewn alleys, crumbling curbs, and vandalized playgrounds of the slums are the badge of the loser in the competition that characterizes urban politics.

Public safety is one of the most coveted conditions which groups want the city to guarantee them. In many neighborhoods, fear stalks the subway stations late at night as gangs of robbers "rip-off" weary drunk stragglers on their way home. Many city residents fear to walk at night because of the mugger who may be lurking in the bushes; they buy triple locks for their apartments to keep the burglar out; they dread the elevator ride that brings them to and from their home because it may trap them in the lockhold of a rapist.

City residents do not only want order; they also seek justice. Justice does not simply involve guarding everyone's safety. It also implies that all legal rights and obligations are respected. For tenants, it means that their landlord abides by city housing and health codes; for people injured in automobile accidents, it means that they receive compensation due them and for buyers that they are protected from fraud. For all urban dwellers it means access to fair judicial hearings when private negotiations fail to resolve disputes. Having these rights and obligations respected is what many residents mean by justice. In this sense law, order, and justice are sought by everyone in the city.

The same conflict that marks the contest for superior schools, trash collections, and streets characterizes the quest for justice. Such conflict is a constant companion to life in the modern city. Residents are often engaged in informal negotiations over faulty merchandise, late payments, unsatisfactory conditions in their apartments, and the myriad of interactions with strangers that require extra effort to obtain their due. Some of the disputes cannot be settled privately or informally. The contestants then run to a lawyer, call the police, or go to city hall. In this book, I am concerned with exploring the elements of city life which condition the quest for justice once negotiations in the network of private associations have failed.

For some of the contestants, justice is not simply a blind execution of the law because they contend that the law itself is an unfair exploitation of momentary or permanent weakness. Law, after all, is the product of dominance in the legislative process or results from advantageously pressing litigation through the courts. People who go unrepresented in the legislature or have been too weak to litigate their claims to appellate courts are frequently unprotected by law.[1]

Moreover, most law is ambiguous in its application at least to some cases. Lawmakers lack the omniscience to foresee all conceivable circumstances. Therefore, the police, other administrators, and courts must use considerable discretion in applying the law. How they exercise their discretion keenly concerns the contestants for order and justice. Many groups expend considerable resources to persuade officials that laws should be administered in ways favorable to their interests. Such persuasion may take the form of a minister speaking to the chief of police about his church's bingo game, which subsidizes the church's activities; persuasion may involve land developers convincing the mayor that zoning laws should be bent in their favor because their development will be good for the city. Persuasion may also simply be a matter of a driver arguing with a policeman that since this is the first time he has run a red light, he should not receive a ticket.

---

[1] Jacobus ten Broek, "California's Dual System of Family Law: Its Origin, Development, and Present Status," *California Law Review*, XVI (1964), 257–316, 900–81; *Ibid.*, XVII (1965), 614–82, is an excellent discussion of the disadvantages that several groups of "disabled" citizens suffer.

When one person or group is given an advantageous interpretation of the law, someone else often pays. The cost may be in taxes assessed against the general community for more dense housing or the hurt felt by some at hypocritical standards of police and churchmen. The cost may be born by consumers who have reduced protection in their dealings with merchants or by storekeepers who suffer greater losses from uncollectable debts. When the police clear a sidewalk on a hot summer night, they do a favor to some residents but the loiterers feel harrassed. What is order for one group may be considered oppression by others; what is considered just by one person may be perceived as exploitation by another. Thus, the quest for justice resembles the quest for many other government services. It engenders conflict in which the benefit of one person is often obtained at the cost of another. Everyone seeks to be a winner, and no one wishes to be among the losers.

The conflict that marks the quest for justice is one of the characteristics that make the administration of justice an element of the political arena. Another such characteristic is that the actions of public officials constitute the principal factors conditioning the quality of justice. The distribution of values—money, honor, or freedom—resulting from the administration of justice is authoritative because it is enforced by the power of the state. People who disregard court decisions may be severely punished. Because the courts possess the power of government, court judgments are eagerly sought. The conflict over justice and the power employed to execute judgments combine to anchor the administration of justice firmly in the center of the political arena.

The form of political conflict, as we shall see in later chapters, is often quite different from what occurs when citizens compete for better schools or better streets. Political parties may play only a marginal role; elections and campaign rhetoric are almost irrelevant to the administration of justice. Instead, interest groups vie for advantageous treatment by currying the favor of the police, by vigorously bargaining in attorneys' offices and court hallways, and by energetically pushing litigation through trial courts to appellate tribunals. Yet, although the forms differ from those ordinarily regarded as political, the conflict over the authoritative allocation of values proceeds as heatedly within legal channels as within election campaigns.

A BRIEF SKETCH OF AMERICAN JUSTICE

The judicial process is a complex one. Although grounded in conflict, it does not follow the familiar routine of legislative or executive action; it also extends beyond the courts themselves.

When two or more persons contend for the same property, accuse one another of unfair dealings, or allege that one inflicted injuries on the other, they may use the legal system to reach an accommodation. When the alleged act involves a crime, the police and public prosecutor intervene between the victim and assailant to bring the matter to court. When no crime is alleged, the persons involved must make their own decision about whether to go to court. This decision will depend on their knowledge of judicial remedies, their ability to pay for court action, and their calculation of the potential benefits of going to court. Most conflicts never reach a lawyer or the courts. Many crimes are not reported to the police or remain unsolved. Even when the police know the offender, no prosecutions may occur for a variety of reasons that we shall discuss later.

The degree of discretion governing decisions to bring conflicts to court establish this phase of the judicial process as a very important one. The conditions affecting such decisions set the agenda of the courts and determine which conflicts will be settled according to the established rules of legal proceedings and which ones will be settled by private norms.

Once a conflict has been brought to court, a wide variety of decision-making procedures are available for its settlement. On the one hand, the case may be adjudicated in open court, which means the matter comes to trial before a judge or jury. The plaintiff (prosecutor or complainant) and defendant submit evidence according to the technical rules of courtroom behavior. The judge or jury decides on the basis of legally admissable evidence where the preponderance of evidence lies. In criminal cases, they decide on guilt if the evidence is convincing enough to show guilt beyond a reasonable doubt; otherwise the defendant is acquitted. In civil cases, the evidence needs only to be preponderant to determine which party is at fault in the proceeding. Adjudications made at trials may be appealed to higher courts.

Most cases brought to court, however, are not adjudicated; they are disposed. The disposition process is much less well known by the general public because it does not take place in open court; it occurs in offices and hallways. It consists of bargaining and negotiation. When criminal cases are negotiated (the vernacular calls it "copping a plea"), the defendant agrees to plead guilty in exchange for a lesser sentence. In civil cases, out-of-court settlements are the preponderant means of disposing personal injury suits and many other actions. Many civil courts have pre-trial conferences, at which attorneys for the two sides are required to meet and attempt a negotiated settlement. In other cases, informal pre-trial negotiations set the stage for the courtroom decision. For instance, uncontested divorces are worked out before the court date and a judgment is agreed upon by the husband's and wife's attorneys. The court hearing then is a mere formality, at which the minimal evidence required to justify a divorce is entered on the record. There is no adjudication but rather a disposition of the case according to pre-arranged agreements. Ordinarily, dispositions cannot be appealed to higher courts.

The third phase of the judicial process involves the execution of decisions reached through the courts. Most people accept the decisions. In criminal cases, they have little choice because the only evasion of a sentence to prison is escape to another locale with the constant danger of apprehension and more severe subsequent punishment. In civil cases, decisions are often accepted because the litigants reached them through negotiation and feel the agreement to be the best that they could obtain, because they have tired of the conflict, or because they think the decision just even though they have lost. However, some civil decisions are evaded or disobeyed, and further court proceedings must be used to compel obedience. The sheriff may be ordered to evict a family; an employer may be told to turn over his employees' wages to the court to pay an overdue debt; a house may be sold by the sheriff because of a defaulted mortgage. In addition, public agencies may try to evade a court order by reinterpreting it or ignoring it—as when a housing authority continues to give preference to local residents over applicants from neighboring towns after a court order to the contrary, or when a city council adopts a councilmanic reapportionment map which does not fully meet a judge's requirements for equal apportionment of councilmanic seats. Such instances require a confrontation between judges and mayors or governors before court orders are executed or forgotten. The consequences of court decisions may be quite immediate, direct, and limited to a single person; or they may have long range repercussions scarcely predictable to the decision-makers. How decisions reverberate through the political arena and social structure varies from case to case. It is another element of variation that is important to understanding the significance of justice to city life and politics.

INTERSECTIONS BETWEEN JUSTICE AND CITY POLITICS

Because most Americans live in cities, the contest for their measure of justice is an urban phenomenon. But that is not enough to make justice an element of city politics. Indeed, justice is rarely listed as one of the services that cities supply. Most of the courts are county, state, or federal agencies and much of the law they apply is adopted by state legislatures and Congress. Nevertheless, the ways in which justice is administered depend heavily on the local political system.[2] Most court personnel are

[2] An earlier attempt to place justice in the urban politics context was made by James R. Klonoski and Robert I. Mendelsohn, "The Allocation of Justice: A Political Approach," *Journal of Public Law*, XIV (1966), 326–42.

veterans of city politics. The flow of criminal cases to the state courts reflects the actions of the city police, who are usually under the supervision of city hall. But these avenues of influence would remain insufficient if the state and federal courts were part of strong hierarchy which forced them to respond to directives from the state capital or Washington. No such hierarchy exists for the courts.[3] The courts lack a chief executive who may issue such directives, and tradition guarantees most judges considerable local autonomy over their courtroom. The absence of state or federal control over urban courts makes courts more responsive to the local milieu in which they operate and in which their personnel are rooted.[4]

Several avenues of influence exist by which city governments can influence the distribution of justice. These avenues include control of the police, involvement in the selection of judges, passage of local ordinances, and promotion of local cultural norms. On the other hand, external constraints limit the influence of local politics on the distribution of justice. These constraints include the imposition of federal and state legislation, external control over court organization and personnel, involvement by outside police forces such as the FBI, state police, and county sheriffs, decisions by appellate courts which are insulated from local political processes, and the effects of the national political culture. Each of these elements requires some further explanation.

Avenues of Influence

The police are the most direct avenue of influence between city hall and the courts.[5] Most police departments operate under the explicit direction of the mayor. The mayor usually appoints the police chief or commissioner, and the city provides the department's budget from its tax revenues. City officials formulate the policies which guide policemen, even though many of the laws police enforce emanate from the state capital.

City police are important in influencing city court operations because the police control the flow of criminal cases to the courts. Private citizens initiate very few criminal cases. If a criminal matter is brought to the courts, it is brought by police officials as a result of their investigation or intervention. Furthermore, the quality of police work defines the limits of court action. Courts cannot return convictions when the police fail to collect sufficient evidence. Courts cannot enforce laws which the police

---

[3] For a consideration of the problems of hierarchy and supervision in American courts see Herbert Jacob, *Justice in America*, 2nd ed. (Boston: Little, Brown & Co., 1972), pp. 145–63; Sheldon Goldman and Thomas P. Jahnige, *The Federal Courts as a Political System* (New York: Harper & Row, Publishers, 1971), pp. 17–48.

[4] Jack W. Peltason, *Fifty-eight Lonely Men*, 2nd ed. (Champaign: University of Illinois Press, 1971).

[5] For a fuller discussion of the role of the police, see pp. 20–32 below.

neglect. Courts cannot punish those whom the police fail to arrest. Consequently, although the courts are often not a formal part of the city government, they depend almost wholly on city police in their administration of criminal law.

The passage of local ordinances has a similarly direct impact on the courts. Local laws, of course, constitute only a small portion of the legal code which may be enforced through court action. But local laws constitute significant attempts by local majorities and controlling elites to influence the distribution of many values. Zoning ordinances, building codes, tax levies, anti-pollution ordinances, and loitering prohibitions are some of the laws which typically are enacted by city councils and challenged or enforced through court action. Each of the regulations—and many others—may alter the distribution of wealth in the city. For instance, urban renewal—which usually requires local legislative approval—typically involves evicting one set of residents and allowing another (generally a wealthier group) to occupy their land sites. The laws which city councils pass constitute an important variable in the agenda facing courts in the city. Courts in cities without anti-phosphate ordinances do not find their courts confronting the detergent industry; cities with strong consumer protection ordinances generate cases that are absent from courts in other cities.

The selection of judges is not always under equally direct influence of city hall. As we shall explain later,[6] there is a bewildering array of procedures used to select judges. But regardless of procedure, it is the rare city whose judges have not had some prior connection with local politics. This is especially true of the judges of state and city trial courts. Such judgeships are usually given to those who have had long careers in local politics—either as active office holders or as behind-the-scenes supporters. These and other selection patterns provide city hall with many channels of communication and influence in the court system. When a ward committeeman becomes a judge, he may sever the public ties to his political party, but he retains an acquaintance with many political activists and intimate friendship with some. He remains sensitive to their concerns and interests. Moreover, city hall officials generally exercise considerable influence over which men become judge and over which courts they shall preside. This power keeps some views from reaching the bench and promotes the ascendancy of others. The consequent influence that city officials exert over the courts is diffuse and may fail entirely in specific cases. But it would be naive to think that courts in the city are independent of city hall.

Finally, city cultures affect the operation of courts in their boundaries. What is the city culture? It is a set of norms which arises from many

[6] See pp. 68–78 below.

sources and makes cities distinctive. For instance, in 1970 at the height of the anti-war sentiment generated by the Vietnam conflict, a Fourth of July parade in Evanston, Illinois, featured several anti-war floats; in other cities, parades by anti-war demonstrators were banned and protestors jailed. In some cities, a traditional culture militates against taking routine cases to court whereas in other cities a more bureaucratic culture promotes their litigation.[7] The predominantly Calvinist, Scandinavian culture of Minneapolis has led to a universalistic, legalistic administration of justice; in Pittsburgh the civic culture of the predominant south and east European, Catholic ethnic groups promotes a more personalized *ad hominen* administration of justice.[8] The laws in these cities are not very distinctive if we look only at the statute books. But if we look at the living law as enforced in the courts, we find that the local cultures have an enormous impact on how courts dispense justice.

Constraints over Local Courts

Local courts are also one of the most important devices through which political activists beyond the city's boundaries exert influence on city affairs. Through the courts, those who are influential in state and federal legislative processes attempt to impose their preferences on city dwellers.

Just as state and national legislation constrains city operations in general, they are also the most apparent external force operating on urban courts. The overt function of courts is to administer the law as it is given to them. Most law even in urban communities is the law adopted by state legislatures and by Congress and interpreted by appeals courts that operate outside the range of direct influence by a single city. City councils play a relatively minor role in legislation and often are authorized by state legislatures to fill only the gaps which the legislatures have left to local option. This limitation exists because cities are still formally regarded as units of the state government; despite an increasing degree of "home rule" powers, state legislatures still regulate many elements of local government in the city. Consequently, city courts are often asked to interpret and apply laws made elsewhere. The city's zoning power is often regulated by state statutes; the city's authority over criminal matters is severely

---

[7] Herbert Jacob, *Debtors in Court* (Chicago: Rand McNally & Co., 1969) pp. 87–96; Robert R. Alford (with the collaboration of Harry M. Scoble), *Bureaucracy and Participation* (Chicago: Rand McNally & Co., 1969), pp. 144–51.

[8] Martin A. Levin, "Urban Political Systems and Judicial Behavior: The Criminal Courts of Minneapolis and Pittsburgh," (Ph. D. Dissertation, Harvard University, 1970). Levin places more emphasis on the political characteristics of the two cities than on the ethnic traits mentioned above.

constrained by the criminal law codes enacted by the state. When merchants seek to obtain court help in collecting bad debts and when landlords apply for a court order to evict a tenant, they are invoking state, not local, law.

The dominance of state and federal legislation in the American legal system has the latent effect of making courts accessible to outsiders who seek to impose their view of the common good on local residents. A city may be composed of a majority of tenants rather than landlords but the landlords' political influence in the state legislature is generally decisive. That influence is translated into laws which give an overwhelming advantage to landlords in the statutes. The courts—even when controlled by city politicians—have little choice but to execute those laws. It may be true that local practices informally moderate the advantage of landlords because local judges delay the hearing of eviction suits or because the local police delay the execution of eviction notices and, therefore, dilute the effectiveness of the eviction remedy for landlords. Nevertheless, the courts act as the conduit of influence from the state legislature to the city arena. That conduit is used by many groups that are more effective in the state or national political arena than they are in city politics. Thus, black minorities in both northern and southern cities have used the courts to gain rights guaranteed them by national legislation and by the federal constitution even though they could not win such treatment through exercise of their influence in local elections and through local officials.

The attempt to influence local decisions through state and national legislation is often blatant and the focus of considerable open conflict in the legislature. State subsidy of urban transit systems hinges on state appropriations. The construction of low-income housing may be restricted by laws which permit ward and precinct referenda. Assessments of local property may be subject to state legislation and regulation. Local judges may be unable to exercise the discretion they would like in handling criminal cases because state legislation does not permit it. Just as frequently, however, the influence of state legislation goes unnoticed and arouses little conflict, but such laws also have a direct effect on citizen and official behavior.

In addition, the courts respond to cases presented by people outside the control of city hall. Most civil disputes involve uninfluential citizens. Even in criminal prosecutions, some cases come to court despite city hall because city governments do not have a monopoly over police forces. Police not under city control supplement the city law enforcement agencies and bring cases of deviant behavior to court; sometimes, such cases are ones which the city police had purposely neglected. For example, where syndicate crime flourishes with the cooperation of local officials, state or federal officials may intervene to drive the syndicate out of town and to imprison local officials.[9]

In most cities, county sheriffs, prosecuting attorneys and the state police exercise independent authority; in all cities the FBI, postal inspectors, treasury agents, and the U. S. Attorney's Office operate relatively free from direct control from city hall. Consequently, local arrangements to overlook some offenses may be ignored by these non-local police forces which independently initiate criminal actions against persons whom they consider offenders. Conflict over the initiation of criminal charges most frequently occurs over vice violations—gambling, liquor, prostitution, and narcotics—which local officials may overlook, either because many local inhabitants do not consider such activities terribly wrong or because the local officials have been influenced by the purveyors of these services to overlook their violations. The state and national police and prosecuting officials respond to different pressures and to different views of morality. Consequently, the courts are used to enforce these extra-local norms.

The national political culture also operates as a constraint on local courts. One element of that national culture is Constitutionalism as expressed by the federal constitution and Supreme Court interpretations of it. Even the most authoritarian city governments find that they must sometimes yield to claims of due process as guaranteed by the federal constitution. Cities possess police powers to preserve peace, but they must use them in ways which do not violate freedom of speech, freedom from unreasonable search and seizure, and freedom of assembly.

Other elements of the national political culture impose themselves on city government through the courts. National norms of racial equality have been imposed on Southern cities through the courts. Without court action, it is unlikely that many Southern cities would have adopted even token desegregation in their schools; the imposition of bussing to achieve desegregation of schools is almost entirely a consequence of judicial action. Similarly, city schools often do not respond to constitutional norms regarding religious celebrations in the schools until court actions force them to do so.

The Significance of Justice to City Politics

Just as city politics may have important consequences for the judiciary, the administration of justice has great significance for life in the city. The courts and the police are the principal means by which people are re-

---

[9] John A. Gardiner, The Politics of Corruption: Organized Crime in an American City (New York: The Russell Sage Foundation, 1970).

assured that government is concerned with their safety.[10] Large cities have always been dangerous, but the visibility of that danger is perhaps greater in late twentieth-century America than ever before because most of the population is literate and can read the scare headlines of the newspapers, and most have television sets and can watch the scenes of horror portrayed by cameras. If Jane Jacobs is correct in her analysis of old and new city neighborhoods,[11] new city communities may be more dangerous than the old ones because they lack the watchful eyes of neighbors who observe strangers and call the police when suspicious events occur. High-rise buildings and suburban tracts are full of blind spots where no one can keep an eye on the neighborhood. Thus, the danger of criminal assault is real for many people and constitutes a major concern of many city dwellers. Safety is one of the qualities of life that city residents demand from their government and the agencies that administer justice have the chief responsibility to provide it.

The quality of justice also affects city life. Some merchants depend on courts to collect their debts; some landlords systematically use the courts to evict tenants whom they no longer wish to have in their buildings. The degree to which such use of the courts is seen as unfair and exploitative by sizable segments of the community becomes part of their judgment of the city as a desirable place to live. Courts process automobile accident claims; and where the delay between filing a case and its hearing is long, some litigants will find justice is denied them. Courts also provide a forum to which citizens may bring complaints against seemingly illegal acts by city officials—such as their failure to reapportion councilmanic districts, their neglect of anti-pollution ordinances, or their plans to build public facilities (such as a sports stadium or an auditorium) on park lands. Such disputes not only directly involve courts in local political controversies, but they also help determine which groups in a city obtain the conditions they consider essential to their comfort and happiness.

INTERCITY VARIATIONS

So far we have been speaking as if all cities were alike and as if we could subsume all city politics and the distribution of justice under one category. Of course, we cannot. There are many variations in cities and

[10] Matthew Holden, Jr., "The Quality of Urban Order," in *The Quality of Urban Life*, ed. Henry J. Schmandt and Warner Bloomberg, Jr. (Beverly Hills, California: Sage Publications, Inc., 1969), 431–54; Allan Silver, "The Demand for Order in Civil Society," in *The Police*, ed. David J. Bordua (New York: John Wiley & Sons, Inc., 1967), pp. 1–24.

[11] Jane Jacobs, *The Life and Death of American Cities* (New York: Vintage Books, 1961).

in the distribution of justice within them. Just as people who move from one city to another "know" that one city (e.g., Chicago) is a better place for them to live than another (e.g., New York), so with careful study it may be possible to identify persistent variations in the distribution of justice and to learn how those variations are related to differences in city characteristics.

No all-purpose classification of cities exists.[12] Economists focus on the transportation facilities and on the industrialization of cities; sociologists focus on population characteristics; medical authorities concerned with public health may focus on both population and climatic conditions.

To understand the relationship between city politics and the distribution of justice, four characteristics distinguishing cities are especially important. The first two are the size of a city and the economic activities that predominate within it. The second pair encompasses the location of the city within a metropolitan area and the relationship between city and county governments.

The number of people and their economic activities are important because these characteristics are associated with the load placed on city courts. Large cities generate more litigation than small ones. Where many people live closely together, reportable crime occurs more frequently than in small towns. Where many people live together, enough commercial activity exists to produce considerable civil litigation—disputes about contracts, land use, or indebtedness. High concentrations of people also bring about more dense concentrations of cars, higher accident rates, and more tort actions seeking compensation for damages and injuries. Consequently, in big cities, there is more business for the courts; the work of the justice-dispensing agencies is salient to large portions of the population.

The level of economic activity however, may moderate the relationship between size and the kinds of demands made on the courts. Poverty and crime are closely related; crime rates are highest in the poorest portions of the city. Consequently, cities with large proportions of poor people are likely to make greater demands on the courts than cities with smaller proportions of poor people. On the other hand, civil litigation is probably related to income in the opposite way. Poor people cannot afford to litigate as readily as wealthier ones. The poor often cannot afford a divorce even though their marriage has dissolved; they do not sue after an auto accident but accept whatever compensation the insurance company offers. By contrast cities with many company headquarters generate more litigation than cities that have only branch offices or plants. Thus, court caseloads

---

[12] For a thorough discussion of classification schemes, see Brian J. L. Berry (ed.), *City Classification Handbook: Methods and Applications* (New York: John Wiley & Sons, Inc., 1972).

are likely to differ considerably in cities according to their economic level and activity.

The second pair of characteristics—the location of the city in the county and the relationship of city government to the county—is important because it structures the response of courts to their case load. Many of the judicial officials are county officials. Where city and county are identical or at least coterminous, the court system is likely to be more closely tied to the city political system. Where the city dominates the county either because of its size or its strong political organization, the relationship is also likely to be close. But where a city is only a small factor in county politics, it is likely to have a smaller impact on the distribution of justice because the inhabitants of the city have no collective means to influence the distribution of justice. Consequently, political activists in central cities of metropolitan areas may have considerably greater influence on the distribution of justice than do their counterparts in the suburbs where the central city is the dominant city in the county. Suburbs may be wealthier and may contain more influentials, but each suburb is only a small part of the county, and its officials are likely to have only a small voice in county affairs. This fact also means they have little influence in the distribution of justice by the courts of the county. When suburbs are in different counties than the central city, suburbanites are restrained from exerting optimal influence on the principal courts of the metropolitan area.

Other kinds of variations also occur. The form of government a city possesses and the degree of partisanship that characterizes local elections may affect the relationship between City Hall and Courthouse. Cities governed by managers which have highly professionalized staffs and low-visibility elections may have a judiciary that is less intimately linked with local issues than cities governed by elected mayors, agencies staffed with patronage employees, and elections managed with highly visible and finely tuned party organizations. How the police are supervised may also bring differences in the flow of cases to the courts.

City-by-city variations occur in the administration of justice at each of the three major phases of the process. There are important variations in the flow of cases to the courts, in the ways by which courts make decisions, and in the consequences of the decisions for city life. At each phase there may be significant links between the judicial process and city politics. City governments are responsible for bringing criminal cases to court; officials who may be closely linked to city affairs make the decisions that dispose of cases in the courts; some of these decisions in turn have a vital effect on city policies or on the lives of many of the city's residents.

Not all city-by-city variations in the administration of justice are linked directly to the city's political processes. In some instances, the linkage occurs most directly in the regulation of the flow of cases to the courts; in other instances, the decisional process provides the most immediate link; in a few the most significant tie between justice and city politics exists in the political consequences of court decisions.

In the following chapters, we shall examine the several stages involved in the administration of justice and the conditions which lead to their linkage with local politics or their insulation from it. We shall also examine how variations in social structure, economic activity, and location contribute to the variations in the administration of justice.

two

CRIME
AND
THE POLICE

Crime is one of the most pressing problems of urban communities. The newspapers report daily murders in large cities, and one spectacular crime after another passes through the front pages. Although there is much academic debate about the meaning of crime statistics, it is indisputable that many people fear crime.

Fighting crime is one of the important services that cities provide, and almost every city has a police department.[1] But American cities vary considerably in how they approach the crime problem. There are great differences in what is considered a crime, how cities organize the police to fight crime, and how the police interact with criminals and with court systems to impose punishment on persons branded as criminals. Moreover, cities differ among themselves as to the incidence of crime and the importance of crime as a social and political problem. All these variations make it fruitless and misleading to generalize about the crime problem and police responses on a national scale. The problem has many local variations and is met in manifold ways.

[1] Cities that do not possess their own police department contract for police services from neighboring cities or from the county in which they are located. The most extensive plan of this sort is the "Lakewood Plan" in the Los Angeles area; see Richard M. Cion, "Accommodation Par Excellence: The Lakewood Plan," in *Metropolitan Politics*, ed. Michael Danielson (Boston: Little, Brown and Co., 1966), pp. 272–80.

WHAT CONSTITUTES A CRIME?

A crime is behavior labeled deviant and considered so dangerous that perpetrators are threatened with punishment legitimately imposed by the government. The behavior may consist not only of actions but also of words, thoughts, or intentions.

The principal manner in which developed societies like the United States declare behavior to be criminal is through statutory enactment of law. The range of behavior which legislators have declared criminal is vast and varies considerably from one part of the country to another and from one period of time to another. In the 1920's, the sale and consumption of alcoholic beverages was considered criminal; this practice still is in a few localities. Until recently, it was considered criminal for persons of different races to be married or to live together in some Southern states. In some states, doctors performing abortions are considered to be engaging in medically sound, socially useful practice; in others, they are considered criminals.

There is general agreement that some activities are criminal. Murder, theft, burglary, rape, assault are universally considered criminal acts in the United States. However, it is not always clear that a particular action falls into the proscribed category. Whether a woman has been raped depends on whether she consented by word or deed. Whether a person attacked another in an "assault" or in "self-defense" depends on the circumstances.

Consequently, it is not behavior itself which is inherently criminal or not. Any activity may be criminal if it is so labeled. What distinguishes criminal from legitimate behavior is the label attached to it.[2] This labelling process occurs in many portions of the political arena. Two aspects are particularly important for our understanding of crime as an urban problem: labelling during the legislative process, and labelling during the enforcement process.

[2] There are other perspectives which define criminal behavior differently. For instance, some scholars and many political activists consider certain types of behavior *inherently* criminal. The definition of crime also may be theologically derived or based on a view of human nature and its inherent virtues and vices. One outgrowth of this view is to perceive crime as a problem involving individual pathology; the criminal needs to be reformed. Another perspective views the seriousness of crime in terms of social perceptions of the injury or damage perpetrated; it generally proceeds from a concensual view of society. The labelling perspective adopted in the following pages does not rest on a consensual view of society nor does it derive its definition of crime from a theological or a naturalistic base.

The Development of Criminal Legislation

The labelling process generally begins with the legislative process. Before the police and then the courts can treat behavior as criminal, they must be given authorization by legislation. The origin of much criminal legislation is obscure. Most has been inherited from previous periods of history. In the United States, much of the criminal code was adopted from English practice and was transmitted from state to state as each was admitted into the Union. Periodically, criminal codes are recodified and reformed.[3]

A few changes in criminal statutes arouse widespread debate. This is particularly true of sumptuary legislation that seeks to regulate behavior on moral grounds about which there is substantial disagreement. The most famous example of such legislation in American history was the prohibition amendment that outlawed the sale of alcoholic beverages in the United States from 1919 until its repeal in 1933. The proponents of prohibition saw liquor as the source of most social evils and thought that its proscription would be an enormous benefit to the country.[4] Many others—although lacking the fervor of the prohibitionists—were equally certain that liquor was not a fundamental evil but rather was the source of considerable pleasure. The debate over prohibition was long and involved a wide spectrum of the public. The debate still continues in localities where liquor sales are prohibited or where the regulation of liquor stores and bars is a perennial political issue. The controversy over the legalization of marihuana has many of the earmarks of the earlier debate over liquor.

But such spectacular debates should not blind us to the fact that most of the lawmaking activity which leads to statutory definitions of criminality is monopolized by professionals in the field.[5] They appear to operate within fairly wide boundaries of public acceptability buttressed by widespread ignorance of the details of criminal legislation. In a study conducted in California in 1968, researchers found that a large majority of samples of the general population, of college and high school students, of high delinquency high school youth, and of youths institutionalized in a California Youth Authority facility did not know the penalties assessed for specific crimes. Most people grossly underestimated

[3] The best analysis of the politics of criminal legislation on which I have relied heavily is John P. Heinz, Robert W. Gettleman, and Morris A. Seeskin, "Legislative Politics and the Criminal Law," *Northwestern University Law Review*, LXIV (1969), 277–358.

[4] Joseph Gusfield, *Symbolic Crusade: Status Politics and the American Temperance Movement* (Champaign: University of Illinois Press, 1963).

[5] Heinz, Gettleman, and Seeskin, "Legislative Politics and the Criminal Law."

the penalties on the statute books even when they had been recently debated extensively in the California legislature. The most attentive and knowledgeable group discovered by this study were adult inmates of a penal institution.[6]

The major participants in the process of legislating criminal laws appear to be persons professionally involved with law enforcement, such as lawyers, judges, police, prison officials, and groups strongly committed to a particular code of behavior, such as church groups.[7] In an ordinary legislative session, changes in the criminal code involve what appear to be only technicalities—changes in the wording of certain statutes, changes in allowable punishments, reclassification of crimes from misdemeanors to felonies and from felonies to misdemeanors. Although each of these changes might involve major social issues if they were perceived in that way, legislators and the lobbyists seeking the changes usually perceive them as "technical" changes around which there ought to be little controversy. The changes made are often designed to assist police, prosecutors, and courts in processing cases; they often come in response to direct requests for such alterations. Their policy implications are rarely discussed in public.

The process by which such changes are proposed and adopted encourage isolation from the wider public. Changes in the criminal code are proposed periodically by commissions of lawyers who specialize in the field. They generally confer with law enforcement officials and with others who have considerable experience in the criminal process. Rarely do such commissions hold public hearings or make an attempt to explain their proposals to the general public. Their recommendations then go to the legislature, where they are generally sent to the judiciary committee. The judiciary committees of most legislatures are predominantly and often exclusively composed of attorneys. Legislative hearings are attended primarily by law enforcement groups and bar associations because few other groups express a concern for such matters. The legislature often adopts the proposals which come out of committee with little debate because other members of the legislature have neither the interest nor the expertise to challenge committee recommendations.

Nevertheless, this process taps some important segments of public opinion and rarely oversteps the bounds of public acceptance. The professionals consulted in the process are not a monolithic group without differences of opinion. Quite to the contrary, they include defense as well as prosecuting attorneys. Not only associations of law enforcement

---

[6] Dorothy Miller et al., "Public Knowledge of Criminal Penalties: A Research Report," in Theories of Punishment, ed. Stanley E. Grupp (Bloomington: Indiana University Press, 1971), pp. 205–26.

[7] Heinz, Gettleman, and Seeskin, "Legislative Politics and the Criminal Law."

officials but also civil liberties groups like the ACLU concern themselves with the legislative process and offer their expert opinions. However, the degree of public acceptance is not just a product of consulting with opposing and differing groups. It is also the product of a general public acceptance of what is law. Few laymen question the legislative or political origins of the law which confronts them. Whatever gaps exist in the consultative process are usually wiped out by the legitimating power of legislative adoption. The formal ritual of a positive vote by the entire legislative body hides the narrow scope of actual consultation and lack of participation from most of the public.

The result is that on some occasions significant segments of public opinion are neglected. The fiasco of prohibition and the widespread violation of marihuana laws indicates incongruities between private norms and public law. Minority subcultures also may run afoul of the law because their normative preferences are not reflected by it. For instance, the law requiring attendance at school is violated by many Amish sects and has led to vigorous and sometimes violent conflict between public authorities and the Amish.[8] Other religious groups—such as the Jehovah's Witnesses, Mormons, and Jews—have also had conflicts with the law because their religious values conflicted with those expressed by public law.[9] Similarly, it has sometimes been charged that criminal codes reflect middle-class white mores and do not represent the value preferences of the poor, the black, and other disadvantaged minorities. The evidence substantiating that charge is largely lacking, in part because many members of the minorities aspire to join the normative community of the white middle class that surrounds them. Nevertheless, some of the apparent lawlessness of ghetto areas is explained by the differences in the norms expressed by the laws and the norms of the local community. Sometimes such differences are even explicitly recognized by law-enforcement officials who use different standards when enforcing the law in the minority locale than in other neighborhoods of the city.[10]

Most laws that define crimes are enacted by state legislatures for the entire state. The authority of cities to enact their own criminal statutes is limited to minor offenses punishable by small fines or short jail terms. Because the legislature acts for the entire state, criminal statutes rarely reflect the peculiarities of life in the various cities of the state. Statutes that outlaw gambling do not distinguish between sidewalk craps and living-room poker; but only the former becomes the object of police action, al-

[8] Harrell R. Rodgers, Jr., *Community Conflict, Public Opinion and the Law* (Columbus, Ohio: Charles E. Merrell Publishing Co., 1969).

[9] *Cf.* David R. Manwaring, *Render Unto Caesar* (Chicago: University of Chicago Press, 1962).

[10] Wayne R. LaFave, *Arrest: The Decision to Take a Suspect into Custody* (Boston: Little, Brown and Co., 1965), pp. 110–14.

though in crowded neighborhoods with poor housing, sidewalks are the livingrooms of many families. Because most criminal statutes are products of legislatures which were dominated by rural interests, rural mores are more clearly reflected by them than are urban values. For instance, penalties for crimes that are common in the city and which may have a different social significance in crowded urban neighborhoods than in rural towns are unusually severe—examples are the maximum penalties for assault, for attempted murder, and for other crimes of violence. On the other hand, no penalties or very minor ones exist for such urban "crimes" as failure of a landlord to keep rats out of his building, shortweighting purchasers of food, or other forms of consumer fraud.

The definition of crime is thus mostly the work of groups outside the city. The laws defining crime, however, provide the starting point for police in the city.

HOW MUCH CRIME IS THERE IN AMERICAN CITIES?

Only part of the labelling occurs during the legislative process. The other part occurs during the enforcement process. Although an act may appear to be within the scope of a criminal law, it is not officially considered criminal unless some law enforcement officer treats it as such.

The principal reason why police do not respond to every behavior that falls within the scope of the criminal code is that the police are unaware of such behavior. Few crimes take place in front of a policeman's eyes. Most crimes occur out of sight of the police. Thieves and robbers commit their crimes when they think the police are far away; assaults and murders are mostly committed inside buildings—either in such public places as bars or in private homes. The police are usually called only after the crime has been committed. But not all victims call the police.[11] When a murder occurs, the police are often notified because the body is discovered or the doctor called in to sign a death certificate suspects foul play. Many car thefts are reported because people often carry theft insurance and must report the theft before they can obtain compensation from their insurance company. But all murders or car thefts do not come to the attention of the police.[12] Many other crimes go unreported in larger

[11] Philip H. Ennis, *Criminal Victimization in the United States*, Field Surveys II, The President's Commission on Law Enforcement and the Administration of Justice (Washington: Government Printing Office, 1967).
[12] Thorsten Sellin and Marvin E. Wolfgang, *The Measurement of Delinquency* (New York: John Wiley & Sons, Inc., 1964), pp. 33–40; Albert J. Reiss, Jr., *Measurement of the Nature and Amount of Crime*, Field Surveys III, Volume 1, The President's Commission on Law Enforcement and the Administration of Justice (Washington: Government Printing Office, 1967).

numbers because the victim considers them too insignificant to involve the police, because the victim is afraid of the police, or because the victim thinks reporting the crime will do little good. The crimes the police do not know about are not counted in official statistics and in a sense did not occur. Consequently, we get quite different estimates from police statistics and from victims' reports about the extent of crime.

One way to estimate the incidence of crime is to search for victims and ask them about the circumstances of the crimes that were committed against them. The most recent such study based on interviews in 10,000 households in 1965 indicates that approximately 6,358 crimes per 100,000 persons occurred during that year in the United States.[13] The finding equals approximately 12.3 million "crimes" during one year. Crime, however, does not occur with equal frequency to all households. Seventy-two per cent of the households reported no criminal incident; the remaining 28 per cent reported criminal incidents. Two-thirds of that group told about one incident, and one-third reported several incidents during the year.[14]

Most of the crimes reported in this survey would be classified as "minor" offenses if they came to the attention of the police. Table 2.1 shows the crime rate for various offenses, with the least frequent listed at the top and the most frequent listed at the bottom. Opinions may vary about the seriousness of some of the offenses. "Malicious mischief or arson" may signify children throwing a baseball through some lady's window as well as setting fire to an apartment building full of sleeping families. Some of the offenses are not usually classified as crimes by law enforcement authorities; for instance, building violations are rarely handled by the police or criminal courts. The data show that, in general, the more serious offenses occur less frequently and the less serious ones occur more often. However, the number of serious offenses is hardly trivial.

Official estimates of crime are much lower. In 1965, the FBI reported only half the number of major crimes which the survey of victims revealed. By 1970, 5.6 million major crimes were reported to the FBI; a survey of victims would probably have revealed well over 10 million major crimes.[15]

Official estimates are so much lower because they are based on the offenses that are known to the police. Many offenses are never revealed to the police. The 1965 survey of households revealed that just under half the crimes which the victims experienced were reported to the

[13] Ennis, Criminal Victimization, p. 8.
[14] Ennis, Criminal Victimization, p. 40.
[15] The American Almanac (New York: Grosset & Dunlap, Inc., 1972), p. 140. Note that The American Almanac is the commercial version of the U.S. Census Bureau's Statistical Abstract of the United States.

TABLE 2.1 INCIDENCE OF "CRIME" ACCORDING TO VICTIM'S REPORT

	Number per 100,000 pop.
Murder	3.0
Soliciting a bribe	9.1
Kidnapping	12.1
Building violations	42.5
Counterfeiting or forgery	42.5
Forcible rape	42.5
Other victimization	51.6
Robbery	94.0
Consumer fraud	121.3
Other sex offenses	172.5
Family	206.2
Vehicle Theft	206.2
Aggravated Assault	218.3
Fraud	251.7
Simple Assault	394.2
Auto Offense	445.8
Larceny over $50	606.5
Burglary	949.1
Malicious mischief or arson	1,061.3
Larceny under $50	1,458.6

SOURCE: Ennis, pp. 9 and 11.

police. Three variables were especially closely related to the decision to report a crime to the police. First, the more serious the crime, the more likely that it was reported to the police. Second, when an insurance claim could be made, the crime was more likely to be reported to the police because recovery from the insurance is often contingent on a police report having been filed. Third, high-income groups were more likely to report crimes than low-income groups. The reluctance to call the police for minor crimes, when no insurance is involved, and among low-income groups is reflected in the reasons given for not calling the police. Three rationales were cited frequently. Most often, people said that the police couldn't do anything about the matter; second most often, people asserted that the incident (although "criminal") was a private affair; the third most frequent response was that the police wouldn't want to be bothered.[16]

Despite the vast number of unreported crimes, the official crime rate rose steeply during the 1960's. The rise of crimes known to the police

16 Ennis, Criminal Victimization, p. 44.

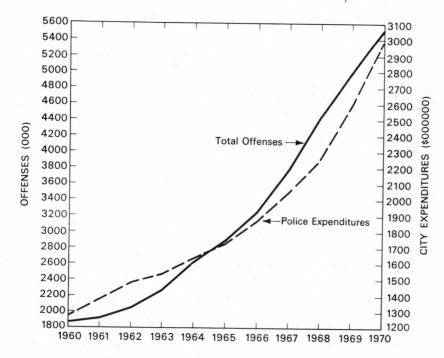

FIGURE 2.1   Total Offenses Known to the Police and
Police Expenditures by City Governments, 1960–70.
(Sources: FBI Uniform Crime Reports, 1960–70; Ameri-
can Almanac, 1972, pp. 140, 415; ibid, 1970, p. 148;
U.S. Bureau of the Census, City Government Finance,
1964–65, p. 5; ibid, 1962, p. 5.)

and reported to the FBI is shown in Figure 2.1. It indicates that the number of violations the police were aware of more than doubled between
1960 and 1970.

Not all cities bear an equal share of the crime burden. Large cities
have more crime. Using only the two crime counts about which there is
least question as to accuracy of the police data—murder and car theft—
we find that there is a close relationship between city size and crime. For
murder, the simple correlation is .82, and for car theft the correlation is .97.
The relationship, however, is not quite so simple: it appears to be ex-
ponential rather than a simple straight line. As Table 2.2 shows, the incidence of these crimes per 100,000 population is much higher in the largest
cities than in smaller ones. In addition, in all cities with substantial numbers of non-whites, the crime rates are higher than in similarly sized cities
with smaller proportions of non-whites. These findings support previous

TABLE 2.2   Crime Rates and City Size, 1969

		Murders/100,000 pop Mean	Car Theft/100,000 pop Mean
Cities	Under 50,000	7.6	352.5
	50,000–99,999	17.6	446.6
	100,000–499,999	15.4	725.5
	Over 500,000	24.6	1218.2
All Cities		12.4	472.3

Source: Based on data published in Federal Bureau of Investigation, *Uniform Crime Report*, 1969.

research which came to similar conclusions based on somewhat earlier data.[17]

These data, however, are somewhat misleading for large and heterogeneous cities. They represent the average for many neighborhoods; some have crime rates comparable to those of small towns while other neighborhoods have far higher rates. Much prior research has shown that reported crime occurs much more frequently in some neighborhoods than others—especially in the slums, where both adult and juvenile crime are abundant.[18] Insofar as such neighborhoods are isolated from the rest of the city, crime rates of large cities exaggerate the danger faced by many city residents and understate the danger posed to slum dwellers.

THE POLICE AND CRIME

The police control almost completely the process by which criminal laws are invoked against offenders. Before cases can come to court, the police must know of violations, investigate them, apprehend those alleged to have participated in them, and collect evidence. Some of those apprehended by the police are not prosecuted—as we shall discuss later—but almost no one who slips by the police enters the courtroom as a defendant in a criminal case.

The police enjoy enormous discretion. If they overlook an offense, the offender is assured his freedom and the fruits of his offense. When the police charge an offense, other authorities are obligated to consider it and the person who is charged faces serious trouble, at least until some

[17] Marvin E. Wolfgang, "Urban Crime" in *The Metropolitan Enigma*, ed. James Q. Wilson (Garden City, New York: Doubleday Anchor, 1968), pp. 270–311.
[18] Karl Schuessler, "Components of Variation in City Crime Rates," *Social Problems*, IX (1962), 314–23.

other official quashes the charge. Probably no other city officials possess such authority over the lives of ordinary citizens.

How this authority is exercised and controlled varies enormously from city to city. The size of police departments is one important element. It is roughly proportionate to the population of the city and its crime rate. The correlation between the number of policemen and city size is .98 for 1969 data. The relationship between the size of police departments and the number of car thefts is equally high. Although some variation exists among cities of similar size, in most cities the amount of money spent on the police is simply a function of the city's size and its associated crime rate.

In most cities, the police department is the largest agency under direct control of City Hall.[19] In cities where the mayor is the chief executive, the police department is usually one of the agencies under his control. The degree of direct control a mayor may exercise depends on his power to appoint the police chief, on the existence of a special police commission which serves as a buffer between the mayor and the police, on the degree to which the police are under civil service regulations, and on the extent to which policemen are unionized. In cities governed by an elected commission, instead of a city council, one of the commissioners (often the mayor) is in charge of the police; his actual authority may also be reduced by other formal arrangements that shield the police from direct supervision. In city-manager cities, the police chief is usually under the manager's supervision although the manager generally must consult with the city council before hiring or firing a police chief. Occasionally, police chiefs must be appointed from civil service promotion lists. These formal arrangements are meant to make the police somewhat responsive to the mandate expressed by the voters at municipal elections and yet remove police from day-to-day politics. Sometimes the arrangements function in that way, especially when "law and order" was an election issue. More frequently, however, the political role of the municipal chief executive produces access points for interest groups who wish to influence police policies.

Except in the smallest cities, police are no longer used as sources of patronage. Entrance into the police force is now a matter of examination.[20] The examinations may discriminate against some groups as Negroes allege, but they do not permit overt use of police positions as a reward for party services. Moreover, many police departments are now unionized, with the consequence that City Hall is perceived by police-

---

[19] The other large agency, schools, is often organizationally independent.

[20] The President's Commission on Law Enforcement and Administration of Justice, *Task Force Report: The Police* (Washington: Government Printing Office, 1967), pp. 125–37.

men as one of the outside groups against which they must protect themselves.[21]

The kind of supervision exercised by police chiefs also varies from city to city.[22] In small departments, there is little formality and little social distance between the chief and his men. As departments grow larger, they become organizationally more complex, with more layers between the chief and the patrolman. On the one hand, the various levels of supervisors are intended to permit the chief to assert effective control.[23] In some cities, for instance, the chief maintains an internal inspection division under his personal control to investigate police wrongdoing and to provide him information independent of the normal chain of command. In other cities, the chief has the authority to promote and demote high ranking members of the department at his discretion, with the effect that they are personally responsive to his wishes. But, as in any large organization, control is difficult because the chief has little personal involvement in the routine business of the department and must depend on information given him by his subordinates.

Control of the police is perhaps more difficult than for other organizations because most of the patrolman's work is unobserved and leaves few traces.[24] He and his partner ride in their patrol car and respond to radio dispatches. No supervisor can observe what they do between radio calls; no supervisor can see what they do when they respond to a call. They may fill out a report which becomes one way of rating their efficiency, but the information they give rarely can be checked. In some areas of their work, their productivity can be measured roughly. For instance, traffic policemen can be rated on the number of tickets they give.[25] On the assumption that many violations occur, traffic patrolmen who fail to give tickets are probably not doing their job. Other kinds of law violations do not occur with the same regularity and predictability. It is more difficult to rate policemen on the number of armed robberies they stop, the number of murders they prevent, or the number of narcotics transactions they discover. Thus, police chiefs must place extraordinary trust in their men; they are able to control only the most flagrant violations of that trust.

The use of discretion also becomes necessary as a result of the am-

21 Hervey A. Juris, "The Implications of Police Unionism," *Law and Society Review*, VI (1971), 234, 235–42.

22 James Q. Wilson, *Varieties of Police Behavior* (Cambridge: Harvard University Press, 1968), especially pp. 57–82.

23 *Task Force Report: The Police*, pp. 42–62.

24 Jerome Skolnick, *Justice Without Trial* (New York: John Wiley & Sons, Inc., 1967); William A. Westley, *Violence and the Police* (Cambridge: MIT Press, 1970).

25 John A. Gardiner, *Traffic and the Police* (Cambridge: Harvard University Press, 1969); Skolnick, *Justice Without Trial*, pp. 76–80.

biguities of the law and the situations policemen encounter. When one man hits another, it is not self-evident whether an assault has occurred or whether it was a friendly tiff. A theft complaint may disguise an attempt to get someone who has legitimately borrowed something to return it. Many calls to the police are to adjudicate marital squabbles; in the course of the fight, a criminal violation may occur, or it may be simply viewed as a private family quarrel.[26]

In addition, the statutes define so many activities as criminal that the police must choose between those which they will enforce. If the police enforce Sunday-closing laws, they cannot be on the lookout for thieves, or they cannot direct traffic near churches and beaches. If they attempt to apprehend every speeder, they cannot maintain surveillance on the local drug dealer.

Discretion, therefore, is a constant characteristic of police work. However, the ways in which it is exercised vary. In some cities, certain criminals are pursued more insistently than others; some kinds of violations are more likely to receive variable treatment than others. Four factors seem to be particularly important in affecting how the policeman's discretion is exercised.

The first factor involves the characteristics of the crime. Some crimes are considered trivial by large segments of the public; others are considered serious. When the police become aware of a serious crime, they have less freedom to ignore it than when they encounter trivial offenses.[27] For instance, when someone reports that his bicycle has been stolen, the police rarely feel obliged to organize a manhunt for the thief. If a policeman is available or if a rash of bicycle thefts has occurred or if the thief is caught in the act, the police may intervene; otherwise, the report will simply repose in the department's files among many other unsolved crimes. But when a murder is reported, the police have little choice but to commit their resources to an investigation. Although the public may tolerate many unsolved bicycle thefts, it is less complacent toward unsolved murders. Another characteristic of a crime which affects police discretion is the degree to which a crime is public. Crimes which occur out of the public's view can be treated with more variable discretion than crimes that occur in full view. The prostitute parading on Fifth Avenue allows the police less choice than the call girl operating out of her fifty-second-floor apartment. A fight that occurs on Main Street at the noon hour can scarcely be ignored while one that occurs in a bar during the supper hour can be treated with greater discretion.

[26] Elaine Cumming, Ian Cumming, and Laura Edel, "Policeman as Philosopher, Guide and Friend," *Social Problems,* XII (1965) 276–86.
[27] Donald J. Black, "Production of Crime Rates," *American Sociological Review,* XXXV (1970), 733–47; LaFave, *Arrest.*

The second factor involves the relationship between the alleged criminal and the victim. The closer the relationship, the more variable the use of police discretion.[28] On weekends, police receive many calls about family fights. They may arrive in the midst of a heated argument in which the husband and wife are ready to attack each other with knives. The police have considerable freedom, however, in deciding their response to such a situation because they know that relationships between spouses vary greatly and that the behavior they are witnessing may not be as serious as it appears. Moreover, they are wary about making an arrest only to discover the next day that the wife is ready to forgive her husband and refuses to press charges. Crimes arising from interactions between a prostitute and her "john" or a narcotics dealer and his customer are often handled with similarly variable discretion. However, when the criminal and his victim are strangers to each other, the police behave with somewhat greater constancy. They are more likely to pursue the case as a matter of policy; there are fewer "extenuating" circumstances that may turn them away from the case.

The third factor is the relationship between the police on the one hand and the criminal or victim on the other. Where the complainant is deferential to the police, the police are more likely to take his complaint seriously than where he is antagonistic.[29] There is also some evidence that the police are more likely to respond to complaints by white-collar persons than to charges made by persons of blue-collar status. Finally, the explicit demand made by the complainant is an important factor in determining police response. The police are more likely to label an event a crime if the complainant is insistent than if he is himself dubious about its criminal character. Since most police actions are in response to citizen complaints,[30] all these elements are significant in affecting how police use their discretionary powers to label a behavior criminal or to write it off as a private conflict.

On those occasions at which the police confront the alleged wrongdoer, the character of their encounter also affects the use of police discretion. The more deferential the accused is, the less likely it is that the

[28] Black, "Production of Crime Rates," pp. 740–47; Cumming, Cumming, and Edell, "Policeman."

[29] Black, "Production of Crime Rates," pp. 740–47. Note, however, that Black's research was conducted only in high-crime precincts in three large cities. We do not know that the relationships described below are similar in low-crime areas of large cities or in smaller cities.

[30] Observers of police behavior often make the distinction between proactive and reactive behavior. The best example of proactive behavior is aggressive patrolling, but it is exceptional rather than normal. Most police behavior is reactive, in response to citizen complaints.

police will arrest him.[31] The more threatening—by word or gesture—the accused is, the greater the amount of force the police will apply to restrain him and the more likely an arrest will be.[32] If the accused is working for the police (as an informer), he may be relatively immune from arrest in minor cases; where the accused has a reputation as a trouble-maker, the police are more prone to arrest him.[33]

Finally, the use of discretion is controlled in part by the policies of particular police departments. These policies reflect the proclivities of the police chief and indirectly the city administration and possibly the populace. The leading student of police discretion, James Q. Wilson, has identified three police styles that characterize distinctive uses of police discretion: the watchman style, the legalistic style, and the service style.[34] The watchman style leads policemen to be most concerned with the maintenance of order. Arrests are made when an incident threatens to become uncontrollable. But if a violation occurs that does not threaten public order, the policeman is likely to dismiss the offender with a warning. Such styles were most evident in New York cities (Albany, Amsterdam, and Newburgh) that had "unreformed" city governments at the time Wilson did his research. By contrast, in other cities, the police take a narrower, legalistic approach. If they are called and the behavior violates a provision of the criminal code, the police more often intervene with an arrest. The policeman is instructed to concern himself with enforcing the law, even when the public order is not disturbed. Such a style characterized Highland Park, Illinois, (a small, wealthy suburb of Chicago) and Oakland, California—both cities with highly professionalized city governments. This legalistic style was in both cases the result of a "reform" police chief assuming office and imposing more stringent control over the use of police discretion. Between these two extremes in police style, Wilson identified a third, the service style. In the service style the police are as responsive to calls from citizens as legalistic departments but handle many complaints as informally as the watchman departments. Service-style departments are especially concerned with maintaining good public relations and police officers are made service

---

[31] This fact also applies to juveniles. See Nathan Goldman, "The Differential Selection of Juvenile Offenders for Court Appearance," in *The Ambivalent Force*, ed. Arthur Niederhoffer and Abraham S. Blumberg (Waltham, Mass.: Ginn and Co., 1970), 156–61.

[32] Jerome Skolnick, "The Police and the Urban Ghetto," in *The Ambivalent Force*, pp. 223–38; Carl Werthman and Irving Pilivian, "Gang Members and the Police," in *The Police*, ed. David J. Bordua (New York: John Wiley & Sons, Inc., 1967), pp. 56–98.

[33] Skolnick, *Justice Without Trial*, pp. 124ff.

[34] Wilson, *Varieties of Police Behavior*.

conscious. Wilson found this style in the relatively homogeneous, middle-class communities of Brighton, Massachusetts, and Nassau County, New York.

In addition, Wilson found that a national sample of cities differed significantly in arrest rates in general accord with his characterizations of police styles.[35] Highly professionalized cities which are most likely to have legalistic police policies have the highest arrest rates in larceny, drunkenness and drunk-driving cases—the kinds of cases that legalistic departments emphasize. Cities that elect their mayor and councilmen on a partisan ballot are most likely to have watchman-style departments which emphasize order maintenance; they have the highest arrest rates in assault cases. However, in situations where the complainant plays a major role—disorderly conduct cases—there are relatively small and inconsistent differences between cities because police department policies have less effect than police-complainant relationships.[36]

Variations in a city are also common. Most frequently they are alleged to be associated with differences in the racial compositions of neighborhoods. Chicanos complain that the police harass them for citizenship papers; blacks assert that the police are more aggressive in dealing with them than with whites, so that respectable as well as poor blacks are stopped, frisked, and questioned routinely in their neighborhood. In part, this alleged discrimination is a reflection of the policeman's occupational culture, which alerts him to the potential dangers posed by those who appear to be different and who challenge the authority of police.[37] According to Westley, the public is seen as "the enemy" by the police.[38] In part, these differences in police behavior also reflect racial prejudice among some policemen.[39]

Although the particular ways in which discretion operates vary from city to city, the effect that police discretion has on the criminal prosecution process is uniform. It drastically reduces the number of cases which actually are brought to the prosecutor and to the courts. In only about 25 per cent of the instances in which someone thinks he has been a victim of a crime do the police label the incident as a crime; in

[35] Wilson, Varieties of Police Behavior, pp. 274–77.

[36] Note that Wilson's research focused on middle-sized cities and did not examine variations in police behavior from neighborhood to neighborhood in large cities. It is likely that such variations exist, at least in some of the largest cities. The more lax attitude of police departments in black neighborhoods may be the equivalent of a watchman style whereas a legalistic or service style predominates in white neighborhoods.

[37] Daniel H. Swett, "Cultural Bias in the American Legal System," Law and Society Review, IV (1969), 81–94.

[38] Westley, Violence and the Police, pp. 48–108.

[39] Ibid., pp. 99–105; David H. Bayley and Harold Mendelsohn, Minorities and the Police (New York: The Free Press, 1969), pp. 144–69.

only 5 per cent of the instances do the police actually make an arrest. As Figure 2.2 shows, half of the attrition results from the failure of citizens to report the "crime" to the police. The remainder of the attrition is due to the failure of the police to respond to the citizen's report to their decision that no crime really occurred, and to their inability to make an arrest.

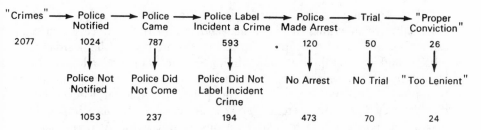

FIGURE 2.2 Attrition Between Criminal Acts and Courtroom Disposition. (Source: Ennis, p. 48. Numbers are numbers of cases in Ennis' sample.)
Note: This figure is based on the victim's knowledge; it is less reliable for arrest and onward since these parts of the crime prosecution process are not very visible to victims of crime.

When the police do not respond to a citizen's call or when they refuse to label the incident as involving a crime, no further action is likely. Almost no criminal cases come to the courts without prior police intervention. Thus, the police sit astride the criminal prosecution process, and whatever happens later in the prosecutor's office and in the courtroom is dependent on what happened on the beat. City residents themselves screen out thousands of cases that may come to the attention of the law; the police screen out additional thousands. Those incidents which do appear on police blotters and lead to arrests are not typical of the lawlessness that may occur in a city. They are typical, rather, of the lawlessness that residents and police consider serious or appropriate for the criminal process. Curiously, these decisions lead to scores of arrests for drunkenness (as Table 2.1 showed)—because no city has adequate alternative procedures or institutions to deal with alcoholism; by default, the police and the lower courts are deluged with these incidents.[40] The cases brought to court reflect scores of individual and institutional decisions

[40] An excellent recent study reviews the variations that exist in police treatment of alcoholics in Chicago, New York, St. Louis, and Washington, D.C. See Raymond T. Nimmer, *Two Million Unnecessary Arrests* (Chicago: American Bar Foundation, 1971).

which are responsive to the pressures we have described. The cases rarely reflect a rational overall policy that seeks to optimize public safety in a city.

CONCLUSIONS

The labelling process characterizing the initial elements of the process by which crimes are identified and criminals are processed gives extraordinary power to people who assert themselves in the legislative process and to the police who administer the standards adopted by legislators. Police control over the initial phases of the criminal prosecution process does not simply give the police the role of gatekeepers, though they certainly exercise gatekeeping powers. It also implicitly makes the police *de facto* judges in many situations. A patrolman's decision not to make an arrest is the functional equivalent of a verdict of acquittal. In many instances, the policeman, however, tempers his judgments with informal sanctions. Those sanctions range from a verbal warning to physical abuse. Because such sanctions are informal and often unauthorized, no records provide a measure of the extent of their application. Journalistic accounts and scholarly research, however, provide many examples and considerable evidence of their existence.[41]

The gatekeeping and *de facto* judging by policemen make the police department one of the most significant bureaucracies in city government. The police in many cities become the target of considerable criticism. In black ghettos where crime is high, opinion of the police is uniformly low.[42] White residents of the central city, where the crime rate is higher, have a greater fear of crime than do suburbanites; they also provide less support for the police in terms of being willing to call them in case of trouble.[43] Cosmetics also have an effect. One scholar has examined the relationship between size of jurisdiction and satisfaction with police services. She has found that in smaller jurisdictions where the police appear to be closely related to the community, satisfaction with police

    [41] Angus Campbell and Howard Schuman, "Racial Attitudes in Fifteen American Cities," in *Supplemental Studies for the National Advisory Commission on Civil Disorders* (Washington: Government Printing Office, 1968), pp. 42–45.
    [42] Harlan Hahn, "Ghetto Assessment of Police Protection and Authority," *Law and Society Review*, VI (1971), 183–94; Bayley and Mendelsohn, *Minorities and the Police*, pp. 110–14; Herbert Jacob, "Black and White Perceptions of Justice in the City," *Law and Society Review*, VI (1971), 69–90.
    [43] John E. Conklin, "Criminal Environment and Support for the Law," *Law and Society Review*, VI (1971), 247–65; note, however, that Conklin's research was carried out only in Boston.

services is distinctly higher than in neighborhoods served by a big city police department with a high degree of centralized control.[44]

There is also some evidence that discontent with the police is associated with dissatisfaction with the quality of life in particular neighborhoods. In Milwaukee, a study of a black ghetto, a white working-class neighborhood, and a middle-class district found that residents had much lower opinions of policemen and the quality of policing in the ghetto than in the white middle-class district; the white working-class area scored in between.[45] When the residents were asked whether "people in this neighborhood are treated as well as people living in other sections of the city?" 40 per cent of the ghetto blacks, 15 per cent of the white working-class respondents, and 7 per cent of the white middle-class respondents answered no. Among black ghetto residents, the three disparities mentioned in explanation of their negative response were better housing, better employment opportunities, and better policing elsewhere. The white working-class respondents answered in terms of better streets and better policing. Clearly, for some residents, policing constitutes a significant element of their estimation of the quality of city life. But as we shall see in later chapters, policing is only one element in the provision of justice in American cities.

[44] Elinor Ostrom and Gordon Whitaker, "Does Local Community Control of Police Make a Difference? Some Preliminary Findings," unpublished paper; Elinor Ostrom, William Baugh, Richard Guarasci, Roger Parks, and Gordon Whitaker, "Community Organization and the Provision of Police Services," Sage Professional Papers in Administrative and Policy Sciences (Beverly Hills, California: Sage Publishers, [forthcoming] 1973); also see buttressing evidence in Campbell and Schuman, "Racial Attitudes," pp. 44–45.

[45] Herbert Jacob, "Contact with Government Agencies: A Preliminary Analysis of the Distribution of Government Services," Midwest Journal of Political Science, XVI (1972), 123–46, presents more details of the Milwaukee study.

three

THE URBAN BAR
AND
CIVIL LITIGATION

Just as the police are the principal gatekeepers regulating the flow of criminal cases to the courts, so the legal profession is the chief regulator of the flow of civil cases. There are, of course, many differences between the bar and the police. The bar is a group of private citizens; they are loosely regulated by the courts in their professional lives, but court supervision of lawyers does not approach the quasi-military control of policemen by their superiors. Although policemen are on city's payroll, most lawyers make their living from fees charged their clients. The police are part of a well-structured hierarchy. The bar is a loosely knit group which shares some professional concerns but rarely exhibits unanimity. Because attorneys are private citizens who organize their own professional ties, they are less responsive to immediate political control than the police. Although characteristics of the legal profession vary considerably from city to city, that variation is not caused by city hall but reflects differences in the economic and social composition of cities.

Consequently, city politics does not exert as direct an influence on the flow of civil cases as in the area of criminal prosecutions. City hall and other governmental agencies have less impact on the initiation of civil litigation. But their influence is not nil. Government agencies help represent persons who cannot retain their own attorneys and initiate or

34

support cases which may otherwise wither. In addition, legislation determines the remedies available to litigants.

Lawyers are the principal gatekeepers over non-criminal cases because almost every litigant seeks the advice of a lawyer before taking his case to court, and almost every litigant must have a lawyer at his side while in court. Litigants need lawyers because court proceedings are governed by innumerable technicalities that laymen are unfamiliar with. The form by which a case is filed, the deadlines that must be met, the motions that may be made, the arrangement of negotiations, the preparation for trial, and the conduct of the trial itself are all matters beyond the knowledge of the ordinary layman. Moreover, the courts assume that all these matters will be handled by lawyers except in small-claims courts, which have very limited jurisdiction. Consequently, the courts have no one assigned to assist the general public as is the case in a tax office or driver's license bureau. The ordinary citizen coming to a court will be referred to a lawyer.

Perhaps it is even more significant that most people do not know what remedies are available through court action. Some remedies—such as divorce—are generally known, but the requirements for obtaining a divorce remain the special knowledge of attorneys. The existence of other remedies—such as personal bankruptcy—are understood by only a very small portion of the population. People with financial troubles may eventually hear about bankruptcy through a friend but the details are understood only by attorneys.[1] Complaints that initiate civil suits and that are sent to defendants are generally written in legal jargon that the ordinary citizen does not comprehend. For instance, consider the summons served on defendants in New York in debt-collection cases. (See Figure 3.1.)

The ordinary person is unlikely to be able to decipher this communication, but he must follow its instructions if he wishes to defend himself against the creditor's claim. Consequently, defendants usually must engage a lawyer who can take the next step in the process. The special knowledge that lawyers possess and its recognition by courts have given them an almost complete monopoly over access to the courts.

That monopoly gives the legal profession control over civil litigation. The control is not exercised by a central body—any lawyer licensed in the jurisdiction may represent any client before a court. But litigants must first find a lawyer before they can think about going to court. Because of the monopoly that lawyers enjoy, the characteristics important in understanding how they control access to the courts are the predispositions that their training produces, the manner in which they offer their services

[1] Herbert Jacob, *Debtors in Court* (Chicago: Rand McNally & Co., 1969), pp. 61–62.

YOU ARE HEREBY SUMMONED to appear in the Civil Court of the City of New York, County of New York, at the office of the Clerk of the said court at 111 Centre Street in the County of New York, City and State of New York, within the time period provided by law as noted below to make answer to the complaint which is annexed hereto; upon your failure to answer, judgment will be taken against you for the relief demanded in the complaint, together with the costs of this action.

Dated, New York, N.Y. _____, 196__

Plaintiff's Address

(Name and Address of
Plaintiff's Attorney)

NOTE: The law provides that:

(a) If this summons is served by its delivery to you personally within the City of New York, you must appear and answer within TEN days after such service; or

(b) If this summons is served by delivery to any person other than you personally or is served outside the City of New York, or *by publication, or by any means other than personal delivery to you within the City of New York,* you are allowed THIRTY days after the proof of service thereof is filed with the Clerk of this Court within which to appear and answer.[2]

FIGURE 3.1   *New York City Civil Court Summons*

to the public, and the conditions which limit public access to legal assistance.

THE TRAINING OF LAWYERS

All American lawyers are now the products of law schools. This was not always true. In the nineteenth century, most lawyers learned their legal skills by apprenticing in a law office. Such apprenticeships, however, have disappeared. In their place, law schools offer the only entry to the legal profession.[3]

Most law schools are appendages of universities, occupying the same

---

[2] Quoted by David Caplovitz, *Debtors in Default* (New York: Columbia University Bureau of Applied Social Research, 1972), Chapter 11, pp. 43–44. Reprinted by permission of the author.

[3] For a historical review of legal education in the United States, see James Willard Hurst, *The Growth of American Law* (Boston: Little, Brown and Co., 1950), pp. 256–76; "Modern Trends in Legal Education," *Columbia University Law Review,* LXIV (1964), 710–34.

position as the school of medicine, of business administration, or of graduate studies. However, a few law schools are independent of universities, and a few are proprietary, for-profit institutions. Most law schools require their students to attend classes during the day and consider their legal training a full-time occupation for the three years it takes to obtain a law degree. A few night schools, however, exist, and permit students to complete law school while they are earning their living at another occupation. Study at night school takes at least four years and often longer.[4]

The curriculum of law schools is remarkably standard, partly the result of the influence of national organizations concerned with legal training which accredit law schools and require substantial uniformity from them. Law students take courses in all the important areas of law—contract, torts, criminal law, property, the Constitution, and court procedure. Although students are now permitted more choice in their second and third years than in the early part of this century, they still do not specialize substantially. Law schools train attorneys who know something about most elements of the legal system and not very much about any particular speciality. Moreover, the curriculum focuses almost entirely on legal doctrine and teaches students to understand legal jargon, to search for precedents and statutes and to organize these materials into acceptable briefs. There is little time for practical experience in dealing with clients, developing evidence, negotiating settlements, or working in a court except through extra-curricular activities. Students get little class work in the psychology of negotiation or the sociology of legal institutions.

The methods used to teach law are also substantially the same throughout the United States. The principal materials are appellate court decisions which have been collected for that use by law teachers. Statutes, administrative codes, lower court decisions, and essays about the law supplement the case materials. From these legal materials, the student is expected to learn how to search for relevant legal materials and how to extract from them the rules which should govern a client's conduct. They are also taught the rationale for these rules, especially as that rationale fits into the web of other laws and rules. To become a lawyer means to learn how to handle legal materials—to find the applicable rule, to know how it applies to your client and how it fits into the larger set of rules and regulations that compose the legal system.

The monopoly that law schools possess in the education of attorneys, the position of law schools in the educational hierarchy, and the curriculum which they follow each contributes to the predispositions that many

---

[4] Joseph H. Tinnelly, *Part-time Legal Education in the United States* (Brooklyn: Foundation Press, 1957).

lawyers display toward the legal process. Those predispositions involve their definition of worthwhile cases, their unwillingness to serve all elements of society, the kinds of remedies they seek for various categories of clients, and the consequences they consider when recommending legal action.

The requirement that prospective law students be college graduates severely restricts the pool of potential lawyers predominantly to members of the middle class. Only three-quarters of the children entering the fifth grade in 1962 actually won their high school diploma in 1970 and 47 per cent entered college.[5] Less than 10 per cent of all 20–24-year-olds had a college degree in 1970.[6] Law school then requires three more years of tuition payments and room-and-board with little scholarship assistance. Most law schools also discourage their students from engaging in part-time work. The out-of-pocket expense of law school is often as high as $4,000 a year and requires the college graduate to forego an annual income of $7,000–$10,000 while he is in law school. The sons and daughters of those Americans who earn less than the median family income usually cannot afford law school; if they go, they normally attend low-status night law schools. As a consequence, the law as a career has become much less a vehicle of upward mobility than it was in the past. Many lawyers who entered the bar during the first thirty years of the twentieth century obtained their training through apprenticeships or by attending part-time law schools which required little previous academic training. This practice brought many sons of immigrants into the legal profession although the bar even then was a predominantly middle-class institution. Contemporary legal education makes the legal profession more of an upper-middle-class institution.

Consequently, most fledgling lawyers come from relatively comfortable circumstances. Their families have had sufficient resources to provide seven years of post-high school education or at least do not need their children's help for the family's support. Very few lawyers are non-white even though law schools have made vigorous efforts to recruit non-white students in recent years.[7] If a young lawyer has an interest in the poor, it is more likely to come from an intellectual concern rather than from personal experience with poverty. Although he may have been exposed to analyses of poverty, racism, slums, or unemployment in college, he is not likely to have experienced these problems himself.

[5] The American Almanac for 1972 (New York: Grosset and Dunlap, Inc., 1972), p. 125.

[6] Ibid., p. 110.

[7] Harry T. Edwards, "A New Role for the Black Law Graduate: A Reality or an Illusion," Michigan Law Review, LXIX (1971), 1432–33.

The familiarity with middle-class standards and inclination toward them is powerfully promoted by the law-school curriculum and the model legal career. Most law courses prepare students to handle business affairs of substantial clients. Courses on contracts and property typically form the core of the first-year program and are the most influential courses in introducing students to the principles of American law. Although some schools now have courses in law and social change, the curriculum is predominantly concerned with the status quo rather than with change. Students are taught the provisions of existing law and the rationales underlying them.

The strong bias of legal education for the status quo and propertied interests also has other foundations. Law as a system of relationships has an inherent bias toward stability and predictability. The legal system is a way of stabilizing social relationships to such a degree that people can deal with one another with confidence; they can predict what others will do because their mutual obligations are relatively stable. In addition, American lawyers obtain most of their income from business clients. The most prestigious law firms are ones with large, corporate clients. Their attorneys earn the highest incomes. In addition, the manner in which ordinary lawyers earn their income makes it highly advantageous to serve the business community. Attorneys with a few large corporate clients who pay them a steady fee are much more secure economically than lawyers who depend on a high turnover of individual clients, each of whom pays a small fee that is not always easily collected. To win financial security, attorneys generally must develop practices which predominantly serve the business community.[8] Therefore, to succeed as a lawyer is to be invited to work for a large firm and then to win a partnership in it. These circumstances are reflected in the required courses and in the courses that students elect in law school.

Consequently, much of legal education is training to serve established interests. Law schools teach their students to keep a steady eye on ways to accommodate their clients' interests with existing laws and institutions. Because the attorney is taught to serve primarily his clients' interests, relatively little attention is paid to questioning the social consequences of prevailing legal practices. Law schools rarely teach their students to become advocates of presently unrepresented interests or to become social engineers in behalf of interests other than the predominant ones. However, distant career aspirations are not the only influence that persuades

---

[8] Jerome Carlin, *Lawyers on Their Own* (New Brunswick, New Jersey: Rutgers University Press, 1962); Jerome Carlin, *Lawyers Ethics* (New York: Russell Sage Foundation, 1966); Erwin O. Smigel, *The Wall Street Lawyer* (New York: The Free Press, 1964).

law students to concentrate on traditional legal subjects. In order to practice law, most students must pass a bar examination.[9] The bar exam focuses on bread-and-butter legal subjects rather than on more esoteric matters. Failure to pass the examination makes the law degree useless for practicing law. About 70 per cent of those who take the examinations pass them; [10] the failure rate is high enough to constitute a real threat to many students and to induce them to concentrate on the subjects on which they will be examined.

THE ORGANIZATION OF LEGAL SERVICES

Lawyers might offer their services like automobile manufacturers, like universities, like physicians, or like none of these. If legal services were organized into a small net of organizations like the automobile dealers, the consumer would have to choose between a handful of trademarked products. Although it might be difficult to judge the quality of each service, advertising might offer hints and motivations, and the oligopolistic character of the market would limit the choice.

If legal services were offered in the same way as higher education, the consumer would have more than 2,000 sources to choose between with a wide range of prices and eligibility rules. The choice would be more complicated than among cars because there is little advertising and there are more sources. Nonetheless, high school seniors know something about the relative reputations of various colleges. They know that Harvard has a better reputation than Sangamon State. The catalogues also tell something about the choice of courses offered and the size of the student body. This information, in addition to the opinions presented by high school guidance counsellors, simplifies choices.

If legal services were organized as the practice of medicine is, the choice of a lawyer would be still more complex. There are more than 300,000 physicians as compared to 2,400 colleges. Moreover, doctors do not advertise and do not send descriptive material to their potential patients. Some work together with others in groups or clinics, whereas others practice alone. However, the telephone directory indicates the specialty of each doctor, so that one does not call a psychiatrist when one needs an obstetrician. But one's choice depends almost entirely on the grapevine and is very much a matter of chance.

[9] A few states admit graduates of approved law schools to the bar without an examination.

[10] American Bar Foundation, 1971 Lawyer Statistical Report (Chicago: American Bar Foundation, 1972), p. 20.

The organization of legal services is like none of these. It makes choice even more difficult than with physicians. There are almost as many lawyers as physicians, but the potential client cannot obtain information about an attorney without visiting him except through friends and acquaintances. The telephone directory does not usually list his specialty; it only gives his location and telephone number.[11] Some attorneys work in large firms with several hundred other attorneys; others work in smaller firms, in partnerships, or by themselves. These circumstances have important consequences for the types of clients they serve and for the quality of service they can provide.

Every large city has a few law firms which concentrate the talents of a hundred or more attorneys.[12] Such firms generally specialize in serving large, corporate clients. Each firm has relatively few clients but each client pays large fees and remains with the firm for many years. Large firms offer a wide range of services in commercial law with a high level of expertise. Except to do a favor for an officer of one of the client companies, such firms do not handle personal cases such as divorce, personal injury, or criminal actions. The large firm is able to provide highly specialized counsel in commercial law because it can assign its attorneys to limited legal specialties and can serve clients with a battery of attorneys rather than with a single lawyer. Few of the attorneys in a large firm go to court; most large firms have a handful of courtroom specialists who handle all court cases. Most of the firms' business involves advice to clients when they negotiate contracts with suppliers, buy real estate, reorganize their corporate structure, negotiate with government regulatory agencies, or seek to minimize their taxes.

Many small firms, some numbering only a dozen laywers, provide similar services to small businesses. The smaller the firm, however, the less specialized the attorneys who provide advice for clients. Smaller firms are more likely to handle personal real estate transactions, personal injury suits, and other cases involving individual rather than business clients. The smaller firms generally have a broader range of clients than the larger ones.

A sizable proportion of the bar works in small partnerships, in shared offices or in solo practice.[13] Such lawyers are the legal counterpart of the medical general practitioner. They handle a large variety of cases, some from small businesses and many from individual clients. Much of their business comes from "walkup" clients who see the lawyer's shingle and

[11] Specialized directories—notably the *Martindale-Hubbell Law Directory*—do provide more detailed information about some attorneys. Although they are available at public libraries, they are not widely known by the general public.
[12] The most detailed description of large law firms is Smigel, *Wall Street Lawyer*.
[13] Carlin, *Lawyers on Their Own* and *Lawyers Ethics*.

wander in with their problem. Many other clients come to them because of acquaintanceships developed in church groups, through lunch clubs, on the golf course, and in neighborhood groups. Many of these lawyers handle much of the business that goes regularly to the courts—personal injury suits, divorce cases, collection suits for local businesses, and personal bankruptcies. Each client pays a relatively small fee (perhaps $250 for a bankruptcy or $500 for a divorce); consequently, lawyers who work alone or in small partnerships must process a large volume of cases.

In addition to these three groups of lawyers who work for fees, many attorneys are salaried employees of corporations and government agencies. Large companies have their own legal departments to handle routine legal affairs. Such departments are the functional equivalent of large law firms, although employment in them does not bring the status of a partnership in a large law firm. Such legal departments are relatively specialized and serve only their own company. Government agencies have similar legal departments to do their law work; cities, for instance, have an office (often called the Corporation Counsel) which provides legal advice to all city agencies and initiates such civil suits as to recover overcharges on supplies bought by the city or to bring a striking city employees union to court in order to end the strike.

A second type of salaried lawyer working for the government provides legal assistance to the poor. In recent years, neighborhood legal aid clinics sponsored by the federal government have begun serving the poor in their slum neighborhoods. The lawyers in these offices provide service in personal cases such as divorces, conflicts with landlords, personal injury claims, and conflicts with creditors.[14] These offices have also provided legal counsel to neighborhood organizations which sought to exercise economic or political power in their areas. Anyone in the neighborhood can come to such an office, and as long as he does not earn too high an income, the office provides free legal assistance. People who can afford to pay are referred to local attorneys—usually ones who are practicing alone or in small partnerships. In many cities, such government-sponsored legal-assistance clinics supplement private legal aid offices which are supported by charities.[15] They too hire attorneys who work for a salary and serve the poor.

[14] Harry P. Stumpf, "Law and Poverty: A Political Perspective," *Wisconsin Law Review*, 1968, pp. 694–733; "Neighborhood Law Offices," *Harvard Law Review*, LXXX (1967), 805. The most detailed financial and case data for offices providing legal assistance to the poor is in *1970 Statistics of Legal Aid and Defender Work in the United States and Canada* (Chicago: National Legal Aid and Defender Association, 1971).

[15] Emory A. Brownell, *Legal Aid in the United States* (Rochester, N. Y.: Lawyer Cooperative Publishing Co., 1951); *Supplement*, (1961). However, by 1971 only 10 per cent of legal assistance funding in the United States came from United Fund, Community Chest or bar association sources. *1970 Statistics of Legal Aid*, p. iv.

ACCESS TO LEGAL ADVICE

The organizational structure within which lawyers work has important consequences for making legal assistance differentially available to various elements of the population. The structure most clearly discriminates against middle-income families.

The varying organization of legal services segregate services to different elements of the population and affects the quality of services offered. Large law firms serve large businesses almost exclusively. Large firms provide the most specialized advice and bring the highest fees. The members of large firms stand at the apex of the legal profession in terms of status and income. Smaller business enterprises receive somewhat less specialized service from smaller firms; their lawyers are likely to have excellent reputations and a high (although not the highest) standing in the legal profession. Individuals receive their legal services from small partnerships and solo practitioners. These lawyers are the least specialized in the legal profession; they also occupy the bottom rungs of the prestige scale among lawyers. Indigents obtain legal advice from neighborhood legal clinics or legal aid offices where the lawyers are salaried and handle only cases involving the poor.

The business community is best served. The presence of large and middle-sized firms provides businesses with a supply of specialized legal advice. Further, businessmen have relatively good estimates of the quality of legal services they are buying. The small number of large firms have developed reputations that can be informally checked. The businessman is also not forced to depend on the knowledge of a single lawyer; when he engages a firm, he knows that he will benefit from the expertise of many attorneys. Furthermore, businessmen are linked to the legal profession in other important ways. Most corporations have at least one lawyer on their board of directors. That attorney can guide the company to law firms that are able to provide the services of the company needs. Businesses do not have to rely on luck to find a competent attorney.

Indigents in large cities are perhaps the next best served from a government agency or charitable office. The lawyers who work in these agencies specialize in their problems. Although many of these legal-aid offices are overwhelmed with cases and even though their attorneys do not have a proprietary interest in any particular client (because they draw their salary regardless of its outcome), indigents have some prior knowledge about the quality of services they may expect. Their choice is quite simple. Either they use the available free clinic or they do without any legal service at all because they cannot afford to pay for the usual fees.

Also well served are people who have cases involving contingent fees, These are usually personal injury suits resulting from automobile accidents. In such cases, an attorney normally charges one-fourth to one-third of the compensation obtained by his client. If the claim is at all promising, clients—regardless of economic status—have little difficulty obtaining legal representation because the lawyer's fee is almost guaranteed. However, the quality of the representation that people obtain depends on their information about lawyers and their success in finding a personal injury specialist.

Middle-income families are worst served and receive the most variable service.[16] They take their legal problems—ranging from assistance in buying a house, drafting a will, obtaining a divorce, settling a disputed charge account, adopting a child—to whatever lawyer they happen to know. Many middle-income people know no lawyers and fail to obtain legal assistance. Many can barely afford the lawyer's fee and postpone their legal problems until the last minute. Some of the attorneys serving middle-income families are excellent; many are insufficiently experienced in the problems presented to them to do an adequate job. Few are specialists. A lawyer mostly handling collection cases or evictions will take whatever divorce case comes to his office. An attorney who handles many divorces will take a personal injury case or a real estate transaction if he happens to get one. These legal problems may not involve difficult questions of law but they do require an intimate knowledge of current practice. There are many nuances to divorce decrees, out-of-court negotiations in personal injury suits, and bargaining over a real estate transaction which the specialist knows but which the occasional practitioner is unaware of.

In addition to these differences in access to lawyers resulting from the organization of legal services, variations in accessibility exist from city to city. The most obvious difference among cities is in the number of lawyers. In large cities, attorneys are numerous enough to support a rich diversity of professional structures. In 1970, for instance, New York had over 55,000 lawyers. Among the largest cities, New York together with Boston, Chicago, Cleveland, Denver, Pittsburgh, San Francisco, and Washington had fewer than 200 residents for each lawyer in the city. Most cities with more than 500,000 population had several thousand lawyers. By contrast, in the ninety-five smaller cities where between 100,000 and 250,000 people lived in 1970, only five had over 1,000 lawyers, and four of the cities attracted them principally because of their status as state capitals. Most of the smaller cities had fewer than 500 lawyers.[17] Many had as many as 800 residents per attorney.

16 Barlow F. Christenson, *Lawyers for People of Moderate Means* (Chicago: American Bar Foundation, 1970).
17 *1971 Lawyer Statistical Report*, pp. 69–71.

TABLE 3.1   NUMBER OF PEOPLE PER ATTORNEY IN 151 LARGEST AMERICAN CITIES, 1970

	Cities by Population		
Persons per Attorney	Over 500,000	250,000 to 500,000	100,000 to 250,000
200 or less	27%	17%	13%
200–499	65%	70%	53%
500–999	8%	13%	24%
1,000 and more	0%	0%	10%
	(26) 100%	(30) 100%	(95) 100%

SOURCE: From data reported in *The 1971 Lawyer Statistical Report* (Chicago: American Bar Foundation, 1972), pp. 59–61.

The reason for the skewed distribution of lawyers lies in the economies of urban areas. Large cities generate more economic activity and have more business concerns which require the services of lawyers. Because most lawyers obtain their income from the services they supply to the business community, they locate themselves where the economy is most active rather than where most people live. In addition, that place is where most of the courts are located. In metropolitan areas, for instance, bedroom suburbs have quite small complements of lawyers. Instead, most lawyers practice in the central city even though they may live in the bedroom suburbs. For instance, Anaheim, California, had only 148 lawyers for its 66,000 people in 1970; the central city (Los Angeles) had 10,000. Likewise, Kansas City, Kansas, had only 284 attorneys for its 168,000 inhabitants whereas the central city, Kansas City, Missouri, had 2,200 attorneys for its 500,000 population. Small cities with high concentrations of business or cities that are state capitals also have relatively many lawyers. In addition to Hartford, Connecticut, with its insurance and state business, other examples are Oklahoma City and Tulsa with large oil companies, and Jackson, Mississippi, Des Moines, Iowa, and Albany, New York, all of which are state capitals.[18]

In smaller cities the bar is not as rigidly stratified as in large ones. In cities with fewer than a half million population, the distinction between large firms and small firms is blurred. There are smaller differences in the income of lawyers, fewer differences in the clients they serve, and more overlap in what lawyers do. One study of a small city in Illinois, for instance, showed that almost all lawyers sometimes handled wills and

[18] Ibid.

probate matters, real estate transactions, and personal injury cases. All but the elite sometimes handled collections, criminal matters, and divorce actions.[19] A considerable portion of even low-status lawyers had a set of regular clients.

If "Prairie City" is typical of other small cities in the United States, the conditions under which legal services are available differs markedly in large cities and smaller ones. In the large cities, the consumer of legal services faces a highly structured legal profession. If the consumer is a large corporation, he can retain a large, prestigious firm. But the best lawyers are unavailable for the ordinary person in trouble with the law or suffering from a legal problem. Such a person has to turn to smaller firms or to a solo practitioner. Individual clients and small business receive less expert legal assistance than large firms in the largest metropolitan areas.

In smaller cities, the best legal services available can be more readily retained by anyone in the city. Even the largest firm may be willing to accept a divorce or a criminal case; the city's best-known lawyer may sometimes appear in court or work on a zoning amendment. However, everyone in small cities receives less specialized counsel.

Another important consequence of this differential stratification of the bar is that in large metropolitan areas, well-known lawyers are unlikely to be active in local politics. Members of the Wall Street-type firm almost never run for local office; one will not even find them as advisers to the mayor or councilmen. Many lawyers are active in politics, but they come from smaller firms and from the ranks of solo practitioners. The best legal talent in the large city remains aloof from local politics. Not so in smaller towns, where the most prestigious lawyer may sometimes seek local political office or may serve as an adviser to local governments. All elements of the bar are involved in city politics in small cities; only the lower two-thirds of the bar are likely to be involved in local politics in large cities.[20]

Still another consequence of the differential stratification systems in large and small cities is the manner in which the Code of Professional Ethics is adhered to by lawyers. The Code is a set of rules which is to guide attorneys. It contains prohibitions as well as injunctions to good behavior. Among the acts which it prohibits is courting pre-trial publicity in the media, splitting fees, using client's funds for personal profit, advertising one's services, helping non-attorneys practice law, and touting one-

[19] Joel F. Handler, *The Lawyer and His Community* (Madison: University of Wisconsin Press, 1967), p. 40.
[20] Contrast Carlin, *Lawyers Ethics*, pp. 11–37 and Handler, *The Lawyer and His Community*, pp. 35–69.

self as a specialist. The rules were formulated by bar associations and have been adopted by state supreme courts and other regulatory bodies. Violations can be punished by revocation of an attorney's license to practice or by lesser penalties, such as temporary suspension or reprimand.

Studies in New York City and in "Prairie City," Illinois, indicate that attorneys in the two locations respond quite differently to these norms.[21] In New York, elite lawyers were the most likely to adhere to the norms; other high-status lawyers were somewhat less likely; the least adherence came from lawyers on the bottom of the stratification system, the solo practitioners. Indeed, elite lawyers may steer to the solo practitioners clients whose problems may require some bending of the norms. Elite lawyers have no economic need to violate the norms prohibiting advertising, touting specialities, or seeking clients (ambulance chasing). They have a well-established clientele which comes to them because of the reputation of their firm. That reputation is spread by word of mouth on the golf links and in other informal ways. Struggling solo practitioners, however, sometimes are pressed to violate ethical norms. One reason so many seek public office is that electioneering provides permissible advertisement of their services. They are also likely to send Christmas cards to former clients and to engage in occasional ambulance chasing to obtain work.

In "Prairie City," Illinois, by contrast, there were few differences between the elite and the bottom of the stratification ladder in adherence to ethical norms. The differences between the top and bottom, as we have already indicated, were not very large. In addition, there were only 118 lawyers in the city (including judges). Every lawyer was at least acquainted with every other lawyer, and a double standard of behavior—one for elite attorneys and another for solos, could not as readily develop. Consequently, most attorneys adhered to the norms prescribed by the bar association. Violations of those norms were considered far more serious breaches of professional conduct than in New York.

The consequence of these differences in structure of the bar and norms of lawyers is that various segments of the population use lawyers with different frequencies. The rich use them more often than the poor, whites use them more than blacks, homeowners use them more than tenants.[22] These differences reflect three related factors: resources with which to employ lawyers, problems that lawyers can help to solve, and organization of the legal profession that makes lawyers available.

These differences in usage are, of course, anchored in variable financial

---

[21] Carlin, *Lawyers Ethics*; Handler, *The Lawyer and His Community*, pp. 73–146.
[22] Leon Mayhew and Albert A. Reiss, Jr., "Social Organization of Legal Contacts, *American Sociological Review*, XXXIV (1969), 308–18.

resources available to potential clients.[23] Lawyers often charge more than $25 per hour for an office visit and for the time they spend on a client's problem. In addition, fees must be paid to courts and to relevant government agencies, and if a court appearance is required, the lawyer's hourly rate doubles. Having an attorney handle the purchase of a house is likely to cost more than $100, and a divorce typically costs at least $250 in lawyer's fees. Even a bankruptcy is likely to cost $125. Consequently, low-income families cannot readily turn to private attorneys for assistance. Only those with some extra money in the bank can use lawyers.

Income differences, however, do not fully explain variations in use of attorneys. A study in Detroit [24] showed that almost 70 per cent of the population had seen an attorney in the previous five years; the difference between rich and poor was that among the poor (with less than $7,000 income) 56 per cent had seen an attorney whereas among the rich (with incomes over $15,000) 83 per cent had seen a lawyer. An additional explanatory factor lies with the kinds of problems that people at different income levels have. Wealthier people have more problems that are traditionally perceived as lawyers' problems. For instance, they are more likely to purchase real estate, make wills, settle estates, or seek advice on business matters. These are problems that only wealthier people have. Wealthier people are also more likely to have high enough stakes involved in a legal dispute to make it worthwhile to hire an attorney. For instance, in disputes over consumer debts, it rarely pays to engage a lawyer when the amount involved is less than several hundred dollars. In fact, the proportion of debtors who use a lawyer in such disputes rises with the amount of money involved.[25] Problems involving large sums of money are also those recognized by the general population and by lawyers as the ones requiring legal assistance. There are fewer social-class differences with respect to other problems such as divorce, or landlord-tenant disputes. The resources which wealthier people have combine with their obviously legal problems to bring them into contact with lawyers much more often than less wealthy families.

LAWYERS AS GATEKEEPERS

The differential access of the public to lawyers and the variations in the quality of service offered to different elements of society have im-

---

[23] See especially Jerome Carlin, Jan Howard, and Sheldon Messinger, "Civil Justice and the Poor," Law and Society Review, I (1966), 9–89.

[24] Mayhew and Reiss, "Social Organization of Legal Contacts."

[25] Caplovitz, Debtors in Default, Chapter 11, p. 71; my own research with debtors did not yield such clear relationships: Jacob, Debtors in Court, pp. 60–62.

portant consequences for the flow of civil cases to the courts. These factors affect both the kinds of cases that come to court and the manner in which they are presented.

Most businesses and persons engaged in conflict prefer to settle their disputes out of court. Even though a suit may be filed, most cases are settled before they reach trial because the litigants prefer to maintain their privacy and wish to avoid the costs of a trial. The preference for out-of-court settlement applies to many businesses just as it does to individuals. Most of the work that lawyers perform for businesses is preventive. Lawyers draft contracts so that the agreements cannot be challenged in court; they negotiate behind the scenes to nip budding conflicts.[26] When businesses come to court, they do so to use remedies which courts alone provide (as in collection cases) or because negotiations have failed. The success that law firms enjoy in avoiding litigation or in negotiating out of court is indicated by the small portion of all cases involving large business concerns. Although big business employs most lawyers, it does not generate most court cases.

Most court cases involve individuals, many of whom are unrepresented by lawyers. A large portion of the routine business of lower trial courts in cities consists of collection and eviction cases. Both typically involve small business firms and landlords who wish to use the facilities of the court to advance their economic interests. In collection cases, the creditors often file "confession of judgments" which the buyer signed at the time of purchase. That confession permits the creditor to go to court unchallenged and obtain a judgment which then can be satisfied by a seizure of the debtor's wages through a garnishment action or by the seizure of the debtor's real or personal property by the sheriff. In most cities, a small group of lawyers specializes in such collection cases. Each case is worth a standard fee of about $10 or a portion of the payment if anything is recovered. These collection agents develop close relationships with court personnel through their regular contact.[27] Debtors almost never appear in court to defend themselves by an attorney. One recent study of collection suits in Chicago, Philadelphia, Detroit, and New York indicated that in Chicago one-third of the debtors had obtained an attorney and in the other cities the proportion only ranged between one-fourth and one-tenth.[28] Debtors lack attorneys because the legal profession is not as well organized to provide them legal assistance as it is to provide creditors with legal services. The latter provides a meager living; the former would have to be charity cases or be subsidized by government.

---

[26] Stewart Macauley, "Noncontractual Relations in Business: A Preliminary Study," *American Sociological Review*, XXVIII (1963), 55–67.

[27] Jacob, *Debtors in Court*, pp. 73–86.

[28] Caplovitz, *Debtors in Default*, Chapter 11, p. 69.

The same thing happens in housing court. Some landlords regularly use the court to assist them in getting rid of tenants they consider undesirable. If the landlord obtains an eviction order, he may get the assistance of the sheriff to break into the apartment and put the tenant's possessions into the street. Without such an order and the sheriff's aid, he may be afraid to take such an action. Landlords are typically represented by attorneys in eviction suits; tenants often are unrepresented. Even if the court rules were relaxed and the proceeding made less formal than it usually is, the tenant would be at a grave disadvantage in presenting his side of the dispute. Moreover, if tenants had attorneys to represent them, landlords might be more cautious about seeking eviction orders and using the court; more landlord-tenant disputes might be settled privately.

Even in cases which do not reach the courts, the absence of legal representation has important consequences for individuals. Most personal injury claims arising from auto accidents are settled before they reach the courts. The insurance company that is liable generally contacts the injured persons and seeks to reach an accommodation with them. The claims agent they send out is often someone who is not practicing law but who has some legal training. He gets a statement from the injured persons which may be used in subsequent court proceedings; he is generally authorized to suggest a compensation payment in return for a release from further claims. Systematic study of these affairs indicates that persons who retain a lawyer are able to obtain much more generous payments (even after the attorney has been paid) than unrepresented persons.[29] The attorney knows much more than the court rules. He may be familiar with the culture of negotiation which characterizes personal injury claims. He can advise his client to seek additional medical attention; he can assure him that if he loses a day's work and pay, that will also be compensated in the final payment. However, only a fraction of those involved in auto accidents are represented by attorneys. Again no systematic mechanism exists to assure that people who wish representation obtain it. It is a violation of legal ethics for lawyers to check hospital lists and solicit clients from among those injured; that practice is called "ambulance chasing" and may be penalized by disbarment. The injured person or his close relatives must have the presence of mind to call an attorney—and then to find a suitable one—before any agreement is reached with the claims agent. Insurance companies, on the other hand, normally staff their claims departments with lawyers or law school drop-outs and, in addition, have substantial legal departments, to take over the cases that eventually reach court.

Legal remedies, therefore, are not used equally by everyone. People

---

[29] H. Laurence Ross, *Settled out of Court* (Chicago: Aldine Publishing Co., 1970).

organized to take advantage of the law—by having legal assistance available to inform them about relevant remedies and about the steps that one must take to obtain them—use the law. Most businesses organize themselves appropriately. Many individuals do not and, therefore, do not take advantage of available remedies.

In addition, new solutions that might be appropriate for alleviating problems of individuals are not developed by the courts because the appropriate cases are often not brought to them. For instance, landlords enjoy a considerable advantage over tenants in the court because they have systematically exploited the legal system to their advantage over the past decades whereas tenants' claims (whatever they might be) have lain dormant. Similarly, the courts have developed effective remedies for creditors, but debtor remedies are not as simply used.

Consequently, a large portion of the population sees the courts and law as principally a concern of business. Many attorneys view the law as principally concerned with property and the propertied. Except for divorce actions, automobile accidents, and the administration of estates, the ordinary man has few occasions under present circumstances to contemplate legal action. The organization of the bar insures that the common man remains a secondary client of the law.

four

OFFICIAL
COURT PERSONNEL

Fourth of July orators like to say that America is governed by laws, not by men. Like all clichés, this slogan has a grain of truth. Laws certainly play an important role in the administration of justice, but men play an even more important one. No laws administer themselves. Courtrooms are not inhabited by self-programmed computers which mechanically churn out decisions. Rather, they are populated by men and women who introduce their own backgrounds, their own biases, and their own preferences into the decision-making process. All are constrained by the law and by each other, but none are automatons.

Those who hold important positions in the courtroom introduce significant inputs into the judicial process. All hold latent or articulated policy views about the administration of justice. Their fear of crime; their view of defendants as educable, ill, or perverse beings; their view of divorce as moral or immoral; their revulsion with debt collection suits or their view of them as legitimate business devices—these and many other policy views may color the use of their discretionary powers.

The policy views of many court officials are rooted in their prior associations with particular groups or with background experiences. Negroes who grew up in the ghetto may remember their childhood experiences with police, criminal courts, debt collectors, and absentee landlords.

Officials who spent their first years in the legal profession working for insurance companies, commercial law firms, real estate management firms, or corporations often internalize the values of their earlier employers and bring them to their courtroom work.

Each official brings to court decisional predispositions. Some officials may have articulated these preferences even though they have made no speeches outlining them explicitly. Others may never have articulated their preferences in public. Although their close friends may know how they feel about crime, divorce, the poor and the rich, no public utterance has recorded these views. Some officials hold firmly rooted and internally consistent predispositions; others have shallow, easily changed, and inconsistent views.

Because officials bring predispositions with them into the court, the kind of men who staff official positions is important to those who contest cases into the legal arena. Just as interest groups may win some advantage by influencing the formulation of law, so they hope to benefit from placing officials who hold favorable predispositions into court positions. However, immediate advantages do not always motivate those who contest court posts. Court offices also convey an aura of legitimacy to the group that wins them. The respect that courts command extends to the principal officials of the judiciary. Consequently, it is a considerable accomplishment and symbolic victory for a group struggling to achieve recognition in the political arena to win a judgeship or to place its man in the prosecuting attorney's office. Such placements connote entrance into the establishment of the political arena.

Three sets of participants attract particular attention in city courts. The most intense struggle is often over the seating of judges because judges occupy the most prestigious office in the judiciary. Almost equally intense conflict surrounds the selection of prosecutors. Public defenders play an important role but are much less visible. A fourth set of officials —court clerks—function with such low visibility that although they may make decisions which affect court outcome, we know little about their recruitment or work.

PROSECUTORS

Prosecutors occupy a central position in the criminal prosecution process.[1] They stand between the police and the courts. No criminal

[1] The prosecutor's title varies throughout the United States. He is commonly called District Attorney, State's Attorney, County Solicitor, Prosecuting Attorney, and United States Attorney.

case can come to court without the prosecutor's approval.[2] The law gives him full discretion. His duty is to prosecute if he believes a violation has occurred and if he can prove it in open court; it is his obligation to refuse prosecution if he believes that no crime has been committed, or if he feels that the available evidence is too weak to prove guilt in court. In many cities, this discretion extends beyond the simple decision about whether to prosecute; it includes the power to decide which charge to press.[3] The police take their evidence to the prosecutor's office with their recommendation but the prosecutor—because of his superior legal skills and his ultimate responsibility to prosecute—makes final decisions about pressing criminal charges.

The prosecutor also controls the grand jury.[4] In some states, the grand jury is routinely involved in making decisions about whether to prosecute by returning indictments or voting "no-true bills." Composed of as many as twenty-three laymen, the grand jury is usually under the tight control of the prosecutor. He is their only legal advisor (no lawyers may sit as grand jurors); he presents evidence to them; he conveys to them his judgments about the likelihood of a successful prosecution. In addition, the grand jury is used in some cities to investigate the operation of government agencies and the possibility of wrongdoing in private and public affairs. The prosecutor also controls the investigative activities of the grand jury. He usually selects the activities which the jury examines. He presents them information which results from police investigations and from the sleuthing of detectives on his staff. Consequently, his office may be used to embarrass one political party or another, to harass an agency with which he is feuding, or to propel him into the public limelight with spectacular revelations.

The prosecutor is also responsible for pursuing all cases to a final determination.[5] His approval is required before a guilty plea may be entered to a lesser offense; such a plea is usually the result of negotiations between him and the defendant's lawyer. Since the prosecutor usually has more information about a case than the defendant's lawyer, the prosecutor normally controls the negotiations. He can make a quick, generous offer or he may delay or even refuse to accept a bargained plea. On the other hand, he must represent the State in all criminal trials. Therefore, he must calculate carefully in order to bring to trial only those cases

2 "Prosecutor's Discretion," *University of Pennsylvania Law Review*, CIII (1955), 1057–81; Albert W. Alschuler, "The Prosecutor's Role in Plea Bargaining," *University of Chicago Law Review*, XXXVI (1968), 50–112.

3 See pp. 96–116 for a more detailed discussion of the prosecutorial process.

4 "The Grand Jury: Its Investigatory Powers," *Minnesota Law Review*, XXXVII (1953), 586–607; Robert Scigliano, "The Grand Jury, the Information, and Judicial Inquiry," *Oregon Law Review*, XXXVIII (1959), 303–15.

5 Alschuler, "The Prosecutor's Role."

which he is likely to win while negotiating or dismissing those he is more likely to lose. His freedom to negotiate permits him to control his public record since little notice is taken of the cases he bargains or dismisses.

In some cities, the prosecutor is also the legal adviser to local government agencies. He is responsible for advising various county-level public boards and commissions and must represent them in court hearings. These civil duties place him in another sphere of action. Although he has much less power in such civil matters, the prosecutor's position in such affairs extends his influence outside the criminal courtroom.

A final function that prosecutors perform is the management of their law offices.[6] In small cities this duty involves only the supervision of a handful of subordinates—an assistant or two, a part-time investigator borrowed from the police, and some clerks. In large cities, however, the prosecutor's office is as large as any private law firm. The prosecutor's office includes many lawyers and a large staff of investigators, often on a loan from the police department but sometimes completely independent of them. The office also includes a small army of clerks who service these professionals. Being a prosecutor in large cities not only requires considerable legal skill and specialized knowledge; it also demands administrative finesse.

These formidable functions make the office extraordinarily attractive for many attorneys. The power in the prosecutor's hands is hardly matched by any other official. Moreover, it is largely unchecked power because review of his decisions rarely occurs. Only when a prosecutor brings cases to court must he confront equally powerful officials who may disagree with his policies. But in addition to sheer power, the position is an attractive springboard for higher office. Few positions so constantly command press space and television time. The investigations which his office initiates are the raw materials of daily newspaper headlines. He occupies a central position in spectacular trials; he controls the dissemination of news on cases which have not yet come to trial. No local office—except the mayor's—may so readily command publicity; none is more adaptable to advancement to a judgeship, a congressional seat, or higher state office.

By contrast, the salary is hardly an inducement to seek the prosecutor's office. Although U. S. Attorneys receive salaries near the median income of lawyers, local prosecutors usually receive much less.[7] Partners

---

[6] John J. Meglio, "Comparative Study of the District Attorney's Offices in Los Angeles and Brooklyn," *The Prosecutor*, V (1969), 237–41; Robert S. Fertitta, "Comparative Study of Prosecutors' Offices: Baltimore and Houston, Ibid., 248–52; George W. Trammell, III, "Control of System Policy and Practice by the Office of the District Attorney in Brooklyn and Los Angeles," Ibid., 242–47.

[7] In 1972, U. S. Attorneys were paid $35,000 annually; local prosecutors' salaries were generally lower.

of equally large private law firms command much higher salaries. Except for being in an advantageous position to make profitable deals in the private sector (for which private attorneys are equally well situated), public prosecutors have few opportunities to become rich. Money is not the attraction; the office lures its occupants with power and with the possibility of advancement.

Two and sometimes three separate prosecutors operate in American cities. The first one is the prosecutor who works in state courts; in most locales he is elected in county-wide elections and serves an entire county. In most instances this means that he operates not only in the central city of a metropolitan area but also in large segments of its suburbs. The second prosecutor is the U. S. Attorney; his office exists in all cities which have a federal district court. The U. S. Attorney is appointed by the President and serves the entire district of the federal trial court. In most states this means that his jurisdiction extends over large portions of the state and usually includes several cities in addition to the one where his office is located. Finally, some cities possess purely local courts which handle violations of municipal ordinances; the prosecutor in such courts is the city attorney who is usually an appointed city official.

With few exceptions, partisan politics plays a controlling role in the recruitment of prosecutors—both U. S. Attorneys and county prosecutors. U. S. Attorneys are considered patronage plums for the party that holds the White House.[8] The term of the U. S. Attorney is four years and often coincides with the President's; when it does not, the customary practice is for the incumbent to offer his resignation upon the inauguration of a new President. The Department of Justice chooses nominees for the position, but they rarely come from the career civil-service staff of the department. Rather, state and local party chieftains make suggestions to the department, and it selects men who merit the post because of their contributions to the party's success or future in the locale where they will work. The appointees are almost always men who reside in the district; they are members of the President's party; they often have held prominent positions in the President's campaign or in state and local campaigns.[9]

The U. S. Attorney's political connections are also indicated by their later careers.[10] In the recent past, fully one-third left their office prematurely for another government post. Most were promoted to significantly higher office with many eventually becoming federal judges, receiving

[8] James Eisenstein, "Counsel for the United States: An Empirical Analysis of the Office of the United States Attorney," Ph. D. dissertation, Yale University, 1968, Chapter 2.

[9] Ibid. Chapter 7.

[10] Ibid. Chapter 7, pp. 33–38.

high positions in the Justice Department, or winning election to Congress. Such patterns are particularly clear for U. S. Attorneys who served in large metropolitan areas. Their tenure was shorter than for small city U. S. Attorneys, and they more often used their position to advance their political career. An extreme example may be found in Chicago, where in this century seven U. S. Attorneys for the Northern District of Illinois became federal judges and two became governor of the state. This element of the post is openly acknowledged by many incumbents. One, for example has said:

> I intend to use my position as U. S. Attorney to do a lot of public relations work. This is ostensibly to build up public appreciation for the office, to instill a respect for law enforcement in the public. But as a practical side-effect, you get to be known in the various parts of the district, and this is an important part of politics. I would be welcome wherever I go to speak.[11]

Their partisan affiliation and activity, however, should not veil the professional qualifications of U. S. Attorneys. All are attorneys, mostly middle-aged. All have had considerable experience in the practice of law, although some have also served in other public office such as the state legislature. Many have had previous experience as an assistant in a prosecutor's office. All are checked by the FBI to assure that they have not themselves been involved in illegal affairs and are considered trustworthy by their associates. They are not, however, formally evaluated by bar associations. They must be confirmed by the Senate, but confirmation is usually a formality.

The Department of Justice maintains continuous contact with the U. S. Attorneys.[12] They are part of the Department's bureaucracy. It provides them with a manual of instructions which they are expected to follow. Difficult or sensitive cases must be referred to Washington, where they are reviewed and where instructions are drafted to guide the U. S. Attorney in his subsequent actions. If Washington disapproves of a prosecution, the U. S. Attorney may not proceed with it. Moreover, some cases are initiated by the Department in Washington. Special "strike forces" to combat organized crime operate from the department's headquarters and control the prosecution of organized crime. Cases involving special expertise—such as anti-trust cases—are also usually handled by attorneys from the Washington office. Thus, although the U. S. Attorneys are political appointees whose claim to office rests on their local partisan

---

[11] Quoted by Eisenstein, "Counsel for the United States," Chapter 7, p. 49. Reprinted by permission of the author.
[12] Eisenstein, "Counsel for the United States," Chapter 4.

contributions, they constitute a part of the Department of Justice's hierarchy and are subject to close supervision by the Department, which is itself usually administered by a close partisan ally of the President.

County prosecutors are even more closely associated with local partisan politics in most cities. In forty-four states, they are elected on a partisan ballot.[13] Unlike many others who are also on the ballot (e.g., judges, county treasurers, auditors, public administrators), prosecutors in big cities often face opposition either in the primary or in the general election. The reason is that the position of prosecutor is one of the most sensitive and powerful in county government. The prosecutor controls much patronage in the form of appointments to assistantships, investigators' slots, and clerical positions in the office; he stands at the entrance gate to the criminal courts and can prevent as well as promote prosecution of any persons who appear to have violated the law; his ability to win press coverage stirs hopes for political advancement.

In large cities, the prosecutor's post goes to experienced politicians. The most serious candidates and the eventual winners are likely to have held prior office. In addition, they have often served as assistant prosecutors earlier in their careers. In most cases, they are firmly associated with the dominant party of their locale. But because the office is countywide, central cities of a metropolitan area do not necessarily control it. Where most of the metropolitan area is in a single county, the prosecutor's post along with other county positions are hotly contested by both parties. In Cook County, Illinois, for instance, Democrats seek the post to protect their city administration from harassment and to use it as a potential weapon against suburban Republicans. Republicans, for the same reasons, urgently seek the post and occasionally win it. In other cities, the county and central city are coterminous, and the prosecutor's office is controlled by the same party that controls the city. For instance, in New York, where each of the boroughs is a separate county, Democrats inevitably control the prosecutor's office in Manhattan, whereas Republicans often control it in Queens and Staten Island. In St. Louis, the city is also a county, giving control of the prosecutor's office to the dominant party in the city—the Democrats; the suburbs are in St. Louis County, and Republicans usually win the prosecutor's office in addition to the other county posts.

Despite the power and prestige of the office, prosecutor's positions are highly valued by only a small segment of the bar. In predominantly

[13] Advisory Commission on Intergovernmental Relations, *State-Local Relations in the Criminal Justice System* (Washington: Government Printing Office, 1971), pp. 113–14. In two states, they are appointed by the governor, in two, by the Circuit Court, and in one (Delaware) the office does not exist.

rural counties with only small cities, the position pays a low salary; the prosecutor is expected to supplement his income with private practice of the law. Consequently, the position is left to young men who wish to make their mark and who can afford to spend some of their time on the public's business because they have not yet built their own private practices.[14] In more urban counties with larger cities, the prosecutor's position is a full-time office, and the remuneration permits one to make a living from it. But in large cities, the bar is highly differentiated, and the most prestigious members of the bar—working in large firms for commercial clients—are inactive in partisan politics.[15] Consequently, few members of the legal elite seek or win the office. Rather, those lawyers active in politics come from the middle- or lower-status ranks of the legal profession. Law is their profession, but politics is their career. They use their legal background to advance themselves politically, or they use politics to advance their law practices. As with U. S. Attorneys, a stint as county prosecutor often leads to a judgeship; it is also one of the most advantageous steppingstones for a statewide, congressional, or national political career as the careers of Thomas E. Dewey, Earl Warren, and many U. S. senators illustrate.

The tenure of elected prosecutors is not usually very long; it rarely extends beyond two four-year terms.[16] Most prosecutors leave their office voluntarily for higher office or for more lucrative private practices. Many prosecutors are promoted by their parties to judgeships. Private practice lures prosecutors, especially in less urban counties because they see their position principally as a platform for building a more thriving legal practice of their own. Only in exceptional cases do prosecutors make a career out of their office.

An important difference between county prosecutors and U. S. Attorneys is that the county prosecutor enjoys almost complete freedom to run his office in any way he chooses within the bounds of the criminal code. He is not part of any larger bureaucratic structure. No state possesses the equivalent of the federal Department of Justice; county prosecutors do not belong to the state's Attorney General's office and are not supervised by him. He provides them no manual of instructions although

---

[14] Herbert Jacob, "Judicial Insulation—Elections, Direct Participation, and Public Attention to the Courts in Wisconsin," *Wisconsin Law Review*, 1966, pp. 809–12.

[15] Jerome Carlin, *Lawyers on Their Own* (New Brunswick, N. J.: Rutgers University Press, 1962); Erwin O. Smigel, *The Wall Street Lawyer* (New York: The Free Press, 1964).

[16] Jacob, "Judicial Insulation"; Kan Ori, "The Politicized Nature of the County Prosecutor's Office, Fact or Fancy? The Case of Indiana," *Notre Dame Lawyer*, XL (1965), 289–303; Richard L. Engstrom, "Political Ambitions and the Prosecutorial Office," *Journal of Politics*, XXXIII (1971), 190–94.

his office may supply expert assistance when (and only when) the prosecutor requests it. The prosecutor is also not part of a county hierarchy. In some locales, another official may wield superior political power. In Daley's Chicago, for instance, there is usually no doubt that Mayor Daley is boss and that the prosecutor (when he is a Democrat) is part of his team. But the prosecutor's subordination in such an instance results from informal political arrangements and not from a formal structure. Consequently, it is more fragile, and in other circumstances, the prosecutor may play a role independent of the city boss or county leader.

Most prosecutor's offices—whether they are county or federal—have substantial staffs of assistants.[17] The prosecutor sets general policy and supervises the operation of the office, but the day-to-day administration of justice is performed by his assistants.[18] Some screen cases as they are brought in by the police; others negotiate with defendants; still others specialize in trial work. Assistantships in prosecutor's offices are often exempt from civil service statutes; in many offices high turnover characterizes many of the posts. The assistantships constitute a significant patronage resource for the prosecutor. All assistants are attorneys; many are young lawyers who wish to gain some experience and to make some contacts before they attempt to establish their own law practices. Because the prosecutor's office is a partisan office, assistantships usually are delivered only to members of the prosecutor's party. This practice means that the aspirant to an assistantship must bring a letter of endorsement from some party activist; he is also often expected to participate in election campaigns.

The largest prosecutorial offices—ones with more than 100 assistants —generally have two kinds of assistants. The first are the young men who hold their position for two or three years and then move to other government jobs or a private career. They are patronage appointees, and their mobility provides the prosecutor with a constant supply of vacancies which he must fill. The second tier—usually in intermediate supervisory positions—is composed of men who have become criminal law experts and who remain in office through the tenure of many prosecutors.[19] Although their posts are not always protected by civil service regulations, their services are so valuable to incoming prosecutors that they retain such experts. This small minority of assistant prosecutors make a career of

[17] Meglio, "Comparative Study of the District Attorney's Office in Los Angeles and Brooklyn"; Fertitta, "Comparative Study of Prosecutors' Offices."

[18] Alschuler, "Prosecutor's Role"; also see Anthony Castberg, "Prosecutorial Discretion," Ph. D. dissertation, Northwestern University, 1968.

[19] Duane P. Nedrud, "The Career Prosecutor," Journal of Criminal Law, Criminology and Police Science, LI (1960–61), 343–53.

their office; they are rarely active in partisan politics and seldom receive promotion to higher public office. But they provide continuity and expertise for the office.

What kinds of predispositions are brought into the criminal prosecution process by these assistants and their chief prosecutors? Although little research has been directed at this question, there are substantial indications that in many cities, most of the assistant prosecutors come from local law schools. In Chicago, for instance, more assistants come from DePaul and Chicago Kent than from the University of Chicago or Northwestern University law schools. They are likely to come from more modest backgrounds than students in elite law schools; they are often graduates of local high schools and colleges and come from families that have lived a long time in the city. The backgrounds of prosecutors suggests that they are particularly sensitive to political implications of their work; they are usually part of the political clique that dominates their locale and, therefore, may be more protective of their fellow officeholders than others would be. When other officeholders are charged with criminal acts, the charges are usually brought by prosecutors who are political rivals or who are autonomous of the local machine. Thus Republican prosecutors may bring charges against local Democrats, or the U. S. Attorney may accuse local officials of wrongdoing. Prosecutors closely linked with other officials rarely accuse them of wrongdoing.

Minority groups are also poorly represented in the prosecutor's office. Although Negroes constitute the largest single ethnic group in many cities, they rarely hold the prosecutor's office and relatively few assistants are black. Moreover, most prosecutors and assistants come from relatively comfortable economic circumstances—as evidenced by their ability to finance four years of college and three years of law school.[20] As most of those accused of crime are poor or black, a considerable culture gap exists between prosecutors and defendants.

The exclusion or "under-representation" of certain groups in the community from prosecutorial positions is an immediate and direct result of the character of the recruitment process. The professional requirements themselves severely restrict the range of potential officeholders. But in addition, lawyers who wish to hold prosecutorial offices must have access through the normal political channels operating in the community. Those barred from political success—because they constitute a political minority (e.g., Republicans in many central cities) or because they do not have adequate representation in legislative or executive bodies

---

[20] In Baltimore, however, where a Negro held the post of State's Attorney in 1972, there were a strikingly large number of black assistant prosecutors.

(blacks in many cities) or because they do not have sufficient resources to engage in politics (most of the poor) are also barred from the prosecutor's office.

DEFENDERS

Every person accused of a crime is entitled to a defense counsel. Most defendants charged with serious crimes now utilize such a lawyer to represent them at negotiations, hearings, and trial.

The position of the defense counsel, however, is very different from that of the prosecutor. How defense attorneys are organized, their influence over the criminal prosecution process, and their political position all differ markedly from that of the prosecutor.

The most apparent difference between defenders and prosecutors is that defenders are not centrally organized into one or two offices in a city. The defense bar consists of many attorneys who operate independently of one another together with a public defender's office that exists in some cities but not all. Defendants hire their own attorney when they can afford it; when a defendant is too poor to engage his own attorney, he may ask the court to appoint one for him. When conviction on the charge may result in imprisonment, the court must comply and appoint a private attorney who has volunteered for such service or an attorney from the Legal Aid Society or from the Public Defender's office if the city has one. Attorneys who handle criminal matters, therefore, do not work under central supervision. Their resources vary considerably. The attorney appointed by a wealthy client may have no limit on his expense funds; he may investigate as thoroughly as he feels necessary to develop an adequate defense. Attorneys for the poor typically have few or no funds for investigation. They must rely on what the defendant tells them and what the prosecutor offers to share with them. The skills of the attorneys also vary considerably. Many lawyers representing defendants handle few criminal cases which are thrust on them. Lawyers who work for a public defender's office and a few independent specialists, on the other hand, are as expert as any member of the prosecutor's staff.[21]

The defense counsel's influence over the criminal prosecution process is fundamentally different from the prosecutor's. The prosecutor plays a gatekeeping function by deciding which cases to prosecute and among them which cases to negotiate and which to take to trial. Defense counsels have much less influence. They are not gatekeepers. They usually

[21] The most comprehensive data are in Lee Silverstein, *Defense of the Poor*, 3 vols. (Chicago: American Bar Foundation, 1965).

become involved only after a case has been initiated; they respond to the prosecutor's decision but cannot veto it. Aggressive and skilled defense may make the prosecutor's work more difficult; it often changes the manner in which the prosecutor handles a case and may alter the outcome of the plea bargaining or trial, but it almost never exerts a systematic effect over the flow of cases to court.

The political position of defense counsel reflects their much weaker influence. First, it is essential to recognize that most defenders are private citizens, not public officials.[22] Even when a lawyer is appointed by the court to represent an indigent defendant, the attorney remains a private citizen. His role is parallel to that of a contractor supplying the government with some service. He works under the same constraints as other private attorneys; he does not report to a bureaucratic superior and is not supervised by any public official. The only exceptions to this rule are attorneys who work in a public defender's office. Such offices are law firms supported by tax revenues or court fees to serve indigent defendants. Their organization is similar to the prosecutor's office, but the recruitment of attorneys is usually quite different. The post of Public Defender is almost always an appointive office; it attracts little publicity and is rarely a springboard for other public office. The constituency which the office serves—the poor and the outlawed—is politically weak. The Public Defender's resources are always insufficient to meet more than the minimum needs of its clients. Attorneys in these offices, therefore, spend all their time and energies keeping up with the cases which have already been assigned them; they have no spare time to meet broader problems aggressively.

Appointments to the public defender's office are usually made by civil service examination. Since the office is less politically attractive, it is less frequently used as a patronage resource. Those who win appointments often use the office as a springboard to a private career as defense counsel; they make many of the same contacts as assistant prosecutors make and eventually have similar private law careers. The office may attract a somewhat higher proportion of lawyers from minority groups or attorneys who empathize with defendants and, therefore, seek out work in this office. But it is unclear whether the backgrounds or predispositions of public defenders are systematically different than of prosecutors.

However, in many cities the public defender's office is organized in such a way that it operates quite differently than private defense counsel. A private defense counsel handles his client's case from beginning to end; he develops familiarity with the case and rapport with his client. In many large cities the public defender assigns his assistants to handle all

---

[22] Defense counsel are considered "Officers of the Court," as are all lawyers, but this position involves no special supervision or political involvement for defense attorneys.

cases in particular courtrooms. As a defendant moves from one courtroom to another during the several stages of his prosecution, a different assistant public defender is assigned to his case. The assistant is often quite knowledgeable and skilled but has little opportunity to build a trusting relationship with defendants. Many defendants do not trust public defenders. It is not unusual to hear one say, "No, I want an attorney," when the judge offers him the services of the public defender.

JUDGES

Judges are the most visible representatives of the justice dispensing apparatus in the United States. Although much of the public is unaware of the other functionaries who work in the courts, almost everyone associates judges with courts. Moreover, judges command the highest degree of prestige and respect in the court system and much more than most local public officials.

Judges perform many important functions, but there is a very large gap between what the public believes judges do or who they think judges are and the realities that exist in the American cities. Before addressing ourselves to the consequences of that gap, we must first examine both the formal and informal functions of judges, and the manner of men brought to the bench by the recruitment process.

Image and Reality

Most people expect judges to be the principal decision-makers. The rituals which take place in courtroom appear to assign them such a role. In criminal proceedings, every person arrested must be brought before a judge within hours of his arrest so that the accused may be told about his legal rights and so that a judge may determine whether he should continue to be held.[23] At the same time or shortly thereafter, a judge sets bail for the accused, determining the amount of money that the accused must pay for his freedom while he awaits trial or deciding that the accused may be set free simply on his promise that he will return for further proceedings (release on recognizance). Later, a judge presides over the arraignment and hears the accused's plea. If the accused pleads guilty, the judge may test the sincerity of that plea. If a plea of innocence is entered, a judge later presides over the trial. If it is a jury trial, the judge decides matters of law—such as whether evidence may be presented—and

---

[23] See David Fellman, *The Defendant's Rights* (New York: Rinehart, 1958); Delmar Karlen, *Anglo-American Criminal Justice* (New York: Oxford University Press, 1967).

instructs the jury about the law before it withdraws to decide the question of innocence or guilt. If there is no jury, the judge himself determines the defendant's guilt. After guilt has been determined through a trial or plea, the judge decides what penalties should be suffered by the accused. Thus, if the script suggested by criminal codes and Supreme Court decisions is followed, judges have many opportunities to exercise decisive influence in the administration of justice.

The same is true for judges hearing civil cases. Lawyers are constantly coming before a judge for decisions which will govern their conduct in a case.[24] They ask him to dismiss the case or accept jurisdiction, to obtain an order requiring the opposing party to disclose its evidence, to postpone or expedite the trial. At the trial, the judge exercises the same powers as in criminal cases—sometimes sharing decisions with a jury but often making them without juries.

In reality, however, this script is not followed; the proceedings are much more complex. Judges operate within constraints established by the law, by their relationship with other officials of the court, by the caseload they must process, and by their own predispositions.

The law establishes significant constraints that remain unobtrusive because they are generally accepted and leave wide bounds of acceptable behavior. In setting bail, for instance, the criminal code usually only states which offenses are bailable and prohibits excessive bail. The law prescribes the hearings that must be held although it does not regulate their contents in minute detail. The criminal code limits sentences by establishing minimum and maximum punishments for most crimes. Judges may not exceed such bounds, but the law rarely imposes insurmountable barriers toward achieving whatever goals judges wish to pursue.

Relationships with other court officials create more imposing constraints on most judges. In the criminal process, judges depend on prosecutors and the police for their flow of cases. Those officials select the cases brought to court; and since the burden of proof rests on the prosecution, they also bear principal responsibility for their presentation. Judges may help bumbling prosecutors,[25] but their potential assistance is limited by their lack of independent information about the incidents that led to the court case. The preliminary decisions that prosecutors make impose especially important constraints on judges. Cases that prosecutors refuse to charge do not reach the judge's courtroom. Those cases which do reach

---

[24] For a formal description of the civil litigation process and the judge's role in it, see Lewis Mayers, *The American Legal System* (New York: Harper & Row, Publishers, 1964), pp. 225–71.

[25] Stephen R. Bing and S. Stephen Rosenfeld, *The Quality of Justice in the Lower Criminal Courts of Metropolitan Boston* (Boston: Lawyers Committee for Civil Rights Under Law, 1970), pp. 29–30, 81.

him have already been processed to a considerable degree. As the prosecutor often depends on a large number of guilty pleas to manage his own
case load, prosecutors often bargain with defendants. When they offer to
reduce the charge, the judge is constrained to accept the bargain because
he has no independent information that allows him to ascertain whether
the lower charge is inappropriate; further, he must work with the prosecutor
for a long period of time and must maintain a smooth working relationship with him. Accepting the lesser charge and accompanying guilty plea,
constrains the judge"s sentencing decision because the law usually prescribes lesser penalties for less serious offenses. At other times, the plea
bargain involves a direct promise for a lesser sentence, a promise that
the judge must honor or risk the withdrawal of the plea. Sentencing
decisions also reflect the judge's information about defendants' backgrounds—information which usually comes from probation officers or
prosecutors.

The caseload imposes its own constraints and reinforces those emanat-
ing from the prosecutor's actions. Most trial courts in urban centers have
woefully inadequate facilities and staff. They cannot try even a fraction of
the cases which are filed in court. When the law requires formal hearings
(e.g., arraignments), the only means by which judges manage to process
their caseload is to hold extremely brief hearings. Arraignments and bail
hearings typically last less than a minute per defendant in trial courts of
large cities.[26] Such swift proceedings force the judge to rely on general
standards and the recommendations of others. In bail hearings, for instance, judges do not normally take into account the circumstances of
the crime or the characteristics of the defendant. The see only the charge
and the defendant's prior record; they consequently rely on a table of
bail requirements which equates particular charges with bail amounts or on
the bail recommendation of the prosecutor or other court official.

All these constraints limit the scope of the judge's discretion in making decisions, but some discretion usually remains. His own predispositions
guide the actions of prosecutors and other court clients in steering cases
to or from his courtroom and in making bargains they know he will accept.
The judge may also insist on his decision-making prerogatives and upset
decisions made by others even though that insistence may make his own
workload heavier or more difficult in the future. Consequently, one may
usually discern differences between judges in sentences they mete out for
particular offenses. Local attorneys who do considerable trial work know

[26] Frederic Suffet, "Bail Setting: A Study of Courtroom Interaction," *Crime and Delinquency*, XII (1966), 318–31; Maureen Mileski, "Courtroom Encounters: An Observation Study of a Lower Criminal Court," *Law and Society Review*, V (1971), 473–538.

which judges are more or less favorable to their kind of case. The discretion that the judge enjoys, however, remains bounded by the law, by other officials' actions, and by the caseload.

Another element of the popular image of the judge is that he decides complex legal issues. His position is portrayed as a challenging one requiring considerable legal skill.[27] This picture is generally untrue. Most trial judges perform routine tasks; their boredom is reflected by the quasi-slumbering posture that many judges display while opposing attorneys present their contentions before the bench. The massive flow of cases through their court precludes anything but a cursory examination of the issues brought to their attention. Judges, like many factory workers, sit on an assembly line. They repeatedly perform routine tasks, with each task consuming only a fraction more than a minute.[28] For such judges, their role is exactly the opposite of the intellectual challenge a judgeship is presumed to pose; it is a mind-deadening, stupefying post.

Judges have another function which is less visible to most of the public. They must manage their courtrooms. They recruit and train clerks, they establish administrative procedures, and they enforce rules of court decorum. In large cities, the courts are staffed by so many judges that these administrative functions have devalued upon a chief judge who devotes almost his entire time to management problems. One element of the management problem is to keep track of the thousands of documents which form an essential part of court files. A misplaced document may mean the loss of a case. Unlike the records of many other governmental agencies, most court records are available for public inspection and are constantly used by attorneys; that use requires a rapid file retrieval system and affords many opportunities for losing documents.[29] However, few courts have brought modern technology to these problems. Most records are still kept in bulky file folders, and case numbers are recorded by hand in bound ledgers. Sears Roebuck can locate the order number for a refrigerator part that was produced ten years ago more efficiently than most courts can retrieve the file of a case introduced four months previously.

Another difficult element of the judge's management role is scheduling his cases.[30] Whether a case is ready for trial does not depend on the judge as much as on attorneys who represent the clients. When a case is

---

[27] See, for instance, Bernard Botein, Trial Judge (New York: Cornerstone Library, 1952, 1963).

[28] Mileski, "Courtroom Encounters."

[29] President's Commission on Law Enforcement and Administration of Justice, Task Force Report: The Courts (Washington: Government Printing Office, 1967), pp. 80–90.

[30] Ibid., pp. 165–66.

called for trial, the attorneys may still be negotiating with each other, or one of them may be trying a case in a different courtroom, or he may simply wish to delay final adjudication. The judge may spur the proceedings by threatening to dismiss the case or to discipline the attorneys, but such tactics can be used only sparingly. Consistent application of such pressure leads lawyers to avoid the judge and may, by aborting negotiations, produce more trials than are necessary. Consequently, much of a trial judge's routine is beyond his administrative control, his life is "hurry up and wait." Although depicted as ruler of his courtroom, he is more often captive of seemingly unmanageable outside forces.

The disjunction between the judge's reputed role and his actual functions varies from city to city and from court to court. In small cities, the disjunction may be smaller because the workload is not as great, and the cast of participants is small enough so that relatively close relationships can develop between them and the judge. Judges may have enough time to deliberate over bail and sentencing decisions. In big cities, the caseload is disproportionately greater, and judges work in teams; there is no single judge of the criminal court but a dozen or more. They deal not with a small set of attorneys but with hundreds from the prosecutor's, defender's, and private counsels' offices. Under the circumstances which govern big-city activities, trial judges are reduced to relatively constrained roles. There is also marked variation from court to court. The case load is more pressing, and courtroom participants are more interdependent in criminal court than in civil court; consequently, judges in some civil courts are less constrained and more nearly approach the functions of the mythical judge. Federal trial judges (judges of the U. S. District Court) perhaps most nearly exercise the full powers of the judge. The federal courts are relatively generously staffed; the cases which come before them are rarely the routine, minor criminal offenses or civil conflicts that deluge state courts. Because federal judges are reputed to be more able, because federal court rules are more flexible, and because important cases often cross state lines, federal trial courts more often handle litigation that requires considerable technical expertise from the judge. Also, a higher proportion of cases goes to trial, so that the federal trial judge spends relatively less time ratifying the decisions of others and more time being a decision-maker himself.

Roads to Judgeships

The selection procedures used to recruit judges reflect the confusion over the work that trial judges perform. On the one hand, there is a strong reform movement to bring more intellectual, "better" quality men and women to the bench.[31] On the other hand, many of the informal practices surrounding the selection process recruit persons with more modest credentials who, however, are probably better suited to the actual functions that trial judges perform.

A bewildering array of procedures is used to select judges in the United States. Figure 4.1 shows the methods used for selecting trial judges by the states and federal government. As the figure indicates, most jurisdictions select judges through a partisan or non-partisan election. However, a growing number of locales use a "merit" selection scheme, and a residual set of states allow the governor, mayor, legislature, or city council to appoint judges.

Judicial elections are generally low-key, low-visibility contests marked by little controversy. Many causes lead to this result. Where the elections are on a non-partisan ballot, they usually occur in the spring, when political fever is at low ebb. Like other non-partisan elections (such as those for municipal office and school board members), few voters go to the polls.[32] When judges are elected on a partisan ballot, their election usually occurs at the November general election, but they are obscured among the many other, more competitive contests.[33] In these circumstances, most attention is directed to the contests at the head of the ticket—for president, for senator, for governor, or for congressman. The contests for judges are lost in the hue and cry over other elections.

In addition, judicial elections are obscure because they lack issues and personalities. It is a violation of judicial ethics to campaign on a platform which promises to make certain decisions in cases that will come before the court.[34] Indeed, it is against judicial ethics to campaign with any great vigor. The candidates are, therefore, reduced to making token appearances at lunch clubs, where they deliver homilies about "law and order" and the virtues of the American legal system. Striking personalities have no opportunity to shine in public; the media's attention cannot be attracted by such humdum campaigns. Consequently, judicial elections rarely capture the voters' attention.[35]

Some states appoint rather than elect judges. In a few of these, the governor makes appointments with the consent of one or both houses

---

[31] Richard Watson and Rondal Downing, *The Politics of the Bench and Bar* (New York: John Wiley & Sons, Inc., 1969), pp. 7–14.

[32] Cf. Robert R. Alford and Eugene C. Lee, "Voting Turnout in American Cities," *American Political Science Review*, LXII (1968), 796–813.

[33] Kenneth N. Vines, "The Selection of Judges in Louisiana," in *Studies in Judicial Politics*, ed. Kenneth N. Vines and Herbert Jacob (New Orleans: Tulane University Studies in Political Science, 1962), pp. 99–119.

[34] Canons of Judicial Ethics, No. 30 (Chicago: American Bar Association, 1970).

[35] This result is true even of a relatively hotly contested race for State Supreme Court positions. See Jack Ladinsky and Allan Silver, "Popular Democracy and Judicial Independence," *Wisconsin Law Review*, 1967, pp. 154ff.

FIGURE 4.1 Formal Methods for Selecting Judges of Trial Courts, by States

Appointment by Executive	Selection by Legislative Body	Appointment by Other Judges	Merit Selection	Non-partisan Election	Partisan Election
ALABAMA (some juvenile judges)	COLORADO (City judges)	ALASKA (magist.)	ALASKA	Arizona	ALABAMA
Delaware	CONNECTICUT*	HAWAII (magist.)	COLORADO	California	Arkansas
GEORGIA (county & city judges)	IOWA (police judges)	IDAHO (magist.)	IOWA	Florida	CONNECTICUT (probate)
HAWAII	MARYLAND (People's court in Mont- gomery County)	ILLINOIS (Assoc. judges)	MISSOURI (St. Louis & K.C.)	IDAHO	GEORGIA
INDIANA (some city judges)	MISSISSIPPI (city police judges)	SOUTH DAKOTA (JoP)	NEBRASKA	IOWA (city judges)	ILLINOIS
MAINE	MONTANA (some police judges)	VIRGINIA (most minor judges)	UTAH	Kansas	INDIANA
MARYLAND	NEW JERSEY		VERMONT	KENTUCKY (circuit judges)	KENTUCKY
Massachusetts	(some magist.)			MARYLAND (Balt. city court)	Louisiana
New Hampshire	OKLAHOMA (city judges)			Michigan	MAINE (probate)
NEW JERSEY	OREGON (city judges)			Minnesota	MISSISSIPPI
NEW YORK (city judges**)	RHODE ISLAND (city judges)			MONTANA	MISSOURI
RHODE ISLAND	SOUTH CAROLINA*			Nevada	NEBRASKA (magist.)
SOUTH CAROLINA (city Judges & magist.)	VIRGINIA			North Dakota	New Mexico
WASHINGTON (city judges)				Ohio	NEW YORK
Federal District (judges & magist.)				OKLAHOMA	North Carolina
				OREGON	Pennsylvania
				SOUTH DAKOTA	SOUTH CAROLINA (probate, some county judges)
				WASHINGTON	Tennessee
				Wisconsin	UTAH (city judges, JoP)
				WYOMING	VERMONT (asst. judge prob., JoP)
					West Virginia
					WYOMING (JoP)

Key: Capitalized states use several methods; where no explanation is given in parentheses, it is the major process used in the state. JoP = justice of the peace; magist. = magistrate

* By legislature, without * by city council

** By mayor, without ** by governor

Source: State Court Systems (Lexington, Kentucky: Council of State Governments, 1970), pp. 10-14.

of the legislature. In others, the legislature formally "elects" judges, but they usually do so after a recommendation has been made by the governor, so that there is little actual difference between the two situations. Few formal constraints surround the appointment process. Some governors consult more broadly than others when considering appointments to the bench, but consultation is optional. Lawyers who would like to become judges may conduct covert campaigns by having friends write the governor to urge their appointment.[36] Normally, local and partisan considerations are important. In most instances, a lawyer must have lived for some years in the community where the judgeship is located and must belong to the same party as the governor.

Many men become judges through such an appointive procedure even where the statutes call for elections. The reason is that the law often gives governors the power to fill vacancies until the next election is scheduled. Thus, when a judge dies or retires before the end of his term of office, the governor is permitted to fill the vacancy by appointment. Many of the judges that governors initially appoint win full terms in subsequent elections. In some states where elections are the formally prescribed means for selecting judges, most judges are in fact appointed because almost all judges leave office before the end of their term.[37] In other states, vacancies occur more rarely, and the governor's power is more limited.

Another hybrid procedure has won increasing acceptance throughout the United States in recent years. It is a plan under which the governor appoints from a list of nominees selected by a commission composed of lawyers and laymen. After serving a part of his term, a judge so selected is put on the ballot in an election that resembles a plebiscite. The electorate is asked whether "Judge X shall remain in office." If a majority of voters concur, the judge serves until the end of his term when, if he so wishes, he is put on another plebiscitic ballot. If the judge is defeated in the plebiscite or if his office becomes vacant for another reason, the governor chooses another name from a newly compiled list of nominees. This process severely restricts the choice of the governor and institutionalizes the influence of bar associations. Legislatures have no role in this selection process.[38]

Federal judges are appointed by the President with the consent of the

[36] John E. Crow, "Subterranean Politics: A Judge is Chosen," *Journal of Public Law*, XII (1963), 274–89.

[37] Jacob, "Judicial Insulation"; Bancroft C. Henderson and T. C. Sinclair, *The Selection of Judges in Texas* (Houston: University of Houston Public Affairs Research Center, 1965); Vines, "The Selection of Judges in Louisiana"; Beverly Blair Cook, *The Judicial Process in California* (Belmont, California: Dickenson Publishers, 1967), pp. 45, 53.

[38] Watson and Downing, *The Politics of the Bench and Bar.*

Senate. The appointive process, however, centers more on the Department of Justice than on the White House.[39] The Deputy Attorney General handles preliminary screening of candidates while the Attorney General makes final recommendations to the President. Senate confirmation is often a formality because influential Senators have been consulted before the formal nominations are sent to the Senate. Senators, in fact, have considerable influence in the selection of trial (U. S. District Court) judges. When a vacancy occurs in his state and when he is a member of the President's party, a Senator has an informal veto over appointments. Some Senators do not like to be involved and abdicate their influence; others guard it jealously and insist that the President appoint someone who has their endorsement. If the President refuses, a Senator may invoke the privilege of "Senatorial courtesy," which usually is a signal for his colleagues to reject the appointment. Individual Senators have much less influence over the appointment of appellate and Supreme Court judges, but their interest in trial judges reflects the large role that district court judges play in the distribution of justice in cities because they handle all cases in the first instance and are influential participants of the urban political establishment.

Consequences of Selection Systems

The various selection systems produce distinctive choices for judge-ships by regulating access to the bench in varying ways. Two consequences are especially marked: the influence of the bar and the influence of politicos, which differ significantly from one system to another.

The organized bar has the most influence in cities where the "merit" or Missouri Plan is used.[40] Although there are many variants of the plan, all of them institutionalize the influence of the bar. The nominating commission always includes representatives of the legal profession who must be consulted. Indeed, as the lawyers on the commission usually are more knowledgeable on judicial affairs than the lay members, they are likely to have more influence than lay members; they are likely to take a leading role in the selection of judges. Experience with the Missouri Plan confirms this expectation.[41] Consequently, where it is used, bar politics has replaced party politics as the most important element of the

[39] Joel B. Grossman, *Lawyers and Judges* (New York: John Wiley & Sons, Inc., 1965); Harold W. Chase, "Johnson Administration Judicial Appointments 1963–66," *Minnesota Law Review*, LII (1968), 965–99; Victor Navasky, *Kennedy Justice* (New York: Antheneum, 1971), pp. 243–76.

[40] Watson and Downing, *The Politics of the Bench and Bar.*

[41] Ibid.

selection process. In Missouri itself, the legal profession has divided into rival camps that compete for seats on the nominating commissions.[42]

The bar also has won a voice in the selection of federal trial judges; bar associations rate nominees for the Attorney General, and he may take their ratings into account. But Presidents appoint some persons rated as "unqualified" by the bar, and the Senate sometimes confirms such nominations.[43] The bar's voice in the selection of federal District Judges is not as powerful as its voice in merit selection systems.

By contrast, the bar exercises only nominal influence over judicial selection where judges are elected or are appointed by the governor or mayor.[44] In most instances, the bar is not consulted and cannot by itself raise a powerful enough voice to veto a nominee. Where judges are elected, bar associations sometimes poll their members and publish the results of the poll. But their recommendations rarely reach many voters, and there is little indication that bar associations' recommendations affect the outcome of the balloting. Such polls are usually exercises in futility.

The influence of politicos—party activists, elected officials, and campaign contributors—also varies from one selection system to another. Their influence is marked in numerous ways, many of which cannot be reliably traced through public records or other documentary research. However, at least two kinds of traces of partisan political influence are evident. The first indicator measures political influence by the prior careers of men selected for trial judgeships. This evidence is summarized in Table 4.1. It shows that trial judges selected through the Missouri Plan and non-partisan elections come much more frequently from "non-political" careers than judges selected through a gubernatorial appointment, legislative election, or partisan election. In addition, the data show that legislative careers are especially important as stepping stones to the judiciary where the governor or legislature have an important voice in the selection process. Where partisan elections govern, former prosecutors are particularly successful in winning judgeships.

The difference between gubernatorial appointment and non-partisan election is especially striking in California, where the formal election system is non-partisan election, but where many judges are initially appointed by the governor to fill a vacancy and then to retain office in an uncontested election.[45] As Table 4.2 shows, significantly more judges appointed by the governor may be classified as "highly politically active"

---

[42] Ibid., pp. 19–42.

[43] Chase, "Johnson Administration Judicial Appointments," p. 897.

[44] Wesley G. Skogan, "Party and Constituency in Political Recruitment: The Case of the Judiciary in Cook County, Illinois," Ph. D. dissertation, Northwestern University, 1971; Wallace S. Sayre and Herbert Kaufman, *Governing New York City* (New York: W. W. Norton, 1960), pp. 543–47.

[45] Cook, *The Judicial Process in California*, p. 49.

TABLE 4.1 POLITICAL AND JUDICIAL EXPERIENCE OF TRIAL JUDGES
ACCORDING TO SELECTIVE SYSTEM

	Appt. % (N = 148)	Legis. % (N = 41)	Merit % (N = 12)	Partisan election % (N = 321)	Non-partisan election % (N = 320)
POLITICAL EXPERIENCE					
Held prior public office	56.8	95.1	16.7	53.6	30.4
Elected law enforcement	39.1	19.2	100.0	78.6	71.7
Legislature	66.2	80.7	—	24.5	22.1

Reprinted from "The Effect of Institutional Differences in the Recruitment Process: The Case of State Judges" by Herbert Jacob in *Journal of Public Law*, Volume 13, Number 1, Copyright, 1964 by Emory University Law School, Atlanta, Georgia 30322. Data are for 1955, the most recent date for which they are available. Reprinted by permission of the publisher.

TABLE 4.2 POLITICAL ACTIVITY OF CALIFORNIA TRIAL COURT JUDGES, 1965

	Elected	Appointed	Total	
Highly politically active	9%	21%	18%	
				Chi Sq = 10.98
Politically active	61%	61%	61%	
				Sig. = .01
No political activity	30%	18%	21%	
N =	(102)	(297)	(399)	

Reprinted from *The Judicial Process in California* by Beverly Blair Cook (Belmont, Calif.: Dickenson, 1967), p. 49. Reprinted by permission of the publisher.

than initially elected judges. The non-partisan character of judges is also apparent in Minneapolis, where the trial judges (elected on a non-partisan ballot) rarely have overtly partisan backgrounds; by contrast, in Pittsburgh, where judges are elected on a partisan ballot, trial judges appear to have close links with local political organizations.[46]

The second indicator of political influence comes from a detailed examination of the recruitment of Chicago judges by Wesley Skogan. He reports that about half the judicial candidates in a recent election were recruited by party leaders and that while considering a race for a judgeship,

[46] Martin A. Levin, "Urban Political Systems and Judicial Behavior: The Criminal Courts of Minneapolis and Pittsburgh," Ph. D. dissertation, Harvard University, 1970.

nearly all the candidates consulted with party leaders.[47] In a city like Chicago, where judges initially win office in a partisan election and where the party organization is powerful, politicos exercise considerable influence over the selection process. They serve as gatekeepers to the bench; attorneys whom they veto have difficulty obtaining a local judgeship.

The same appears true for cities where the mayor appoints some judges while others are subject to partisan election. Note, for instance the case of New York, about which one study concluded:

> Among the judges sitting in 1958, not only were there individuals who once occupied comparatively minor posts in one or another of the branches and levels of government, but there are also former congressmen, an ex-Mayor, former District Attorneys, a former Borough President, a former Deputy Mayor, and at least two former city department heads. For others, the courts have been primarily safe way-stations on the road to other political offices. In recent years two judges have left the bench to run for Mayor, and others have resigned to accept other appointive offices, or to seek other elective offices. Six of the fourteen men who have been Mayor or Acting Mayor of the Greater City since its formation in 1898 were judges at some point in their prior careers, and several moved directly from the bench to City Hall. Judicial office thus functions as both a fitting climax to a life in politics and as a snug niche in which to bide one's time.[48]

Differences in access produced by different selection systems produce somewhat different judges; the effects are accentuated by differences between densely populated areas and suburban small-city judicial districts. Table 4.3 shows some of these effects by contrasting the backgrounds of rural, urban, and "highly urban" trial judges in selected states. All the systems produce many judges who are "locals." But the degree of localism is greater for partisanly elected and appointed judges in small cities, where their courts also serve a considerable hinterland, than for judges in rural areas or core centers of metropolitan areas. In addition, the data show that men who attended low-prestige law schools much more frequently come to the bench in highly urban areas when they are appointed or elected in a partisan election than in rural areas or where they are elected on a nonpartisan ballot. Supporting this finding, Skogan shows that a high proportion of judicial candidates are drawn from legal careers in which they practiced by themselves or in small law firms.[49]

A similar geographic bias occurs where the merit system exists and is

---

[47] Skogan, "Party and Constituency," p. 91.

[48] Sayre and Kaufman, *Governing New York City*, p. 535. Reprinted by permission of the publisher.

[49] Skogan, "Party and Constituency."

TABLE 4.3 LOCALISM AND LEGAL EDUCATION OF TRIAL JUDGES
HOLDING A LAW DEGREE

	Appointed	Partisan Election	Nonpartisan Election
Per Cent Judges Born in District			
Rural	29.6 (27)	51.4 (103)	16.0 (94)
Urban	43.9 (57)	60.6 (94)	12.0 (83)
Highly Urban	34.4 (64)	50.0 (124)	3.9 (152)
Per Cent Graduating from Low Prestige Law Schools			
Rural	18.5 (27)	7.8 (103)	0 (94)
Urban	19.3 (57)	12.8 (94)	0 (83)
Highly Urban	40.6 (64)	34.7 (124)	3.3 (152)

* The categories are defined as follows:
  rural   = 0–49.9% urban by 1950 census
  urban   = 50–79.9% urban by 1950 census
  highly urban = 80–100% urban by 1950 census

(Totals are given in parentheses. Legislative and Missouri plan selection are
omitted since the number of judges was too small to permit meaningful
cross-tabulation.)

Reprinted from "The Effect of Institutional Differences in the Recruitment Process:
The Case of State Judges" by Herbert Jacob, in *Journal of Public Law*, Vol. 13, No. 1,
Copyright 1964 by Emory University Law School, Atlanta, Georgia 30322. Data are
on judges sitting in 1955, the most recent data for which they are available. Reprinted by permission of the publisher.

coupled with stringent residential requirements. In Missouri, for instance,
judges in the city of St. Louis must be residents. This requirement eliminates from consideration a large proportion of lawyers who work in large
firms, of lawyers who studied in prestige law schools, and of lawyers
under the age of fifty-five. Lawyers with these characteristics are more
likely to live in suburban St. Louis County than in the city, and their
county residence eliminates them from consideration.[50]

In addition, the selections systems have some biases in common.
They select almost no women and very few Negroes. To a considerable
extent, this practice reflects the paucity of women and blacks in the legal
profession. For instance, in 1965 Texas had only fifty-nine black lawyers,
about .5 per cent of the total bar; none was a judge. Likewise, only 1.7
per cent of the total bar were women, and only two served as judge.[51]

Another common characteristic of these selection systems is that

[50] Watson and Downing, *The Politics of the Bench and Bar*, pp. 50–54.
[51] Henderson and Sinclair, *The Selection of Judges in Texas*, pp. 65–66.

they are associated with long tenure for judges. The formal terms of office vary considerably. Elected trial judges have terms as short as four years and rarely longer than eight years; appointed judges often have terms as long as ten years and in many instances for life (during good behavior). Federal district judges fall in the latter category. Despite these differences in terms to which judges are elected or are appointed, in practice most trial judges serve for life, until they receive higher office or until they tire of their post. Even where elections occur, very few incumbent judges lose their seats as the result of an election contest. In fact, few incumbents even face opposition on the ballot after having won one or two terms against opposition.[52] Judges appointed for a specific period of years are also almost certain to win re-appointment, even when the governor is a member of the opposing party. Consequently, judges hold their offices as long as they wish. As most judges ascend to the bench in their late forties or early fifties, they generally hold office for fifteen to twenty years.

Because electoral defeat or failure to win reappointment is so rare, other means of removing judges have been developed. One important provision has been the establishment of generous retirement systems which induce judges who hold life tenure to retire when they become eligible for their pension.[53] Such provisions—especially in the federal courts—have increased turnover considerably. In addition, judges may be removed in every state through impeachment proceedings, but that seldom happens. Impeachment is an awkward process, requiring full attention from the legislature for several weeks and involving it in an ugly conflict. Modern legislatures are too busy to take time for the impeachment of a trial judge. Many states, therefore, have developed entirely new removal provisions.[54] They usually involve a hearing before the state's highest court or a specially convened group of judges. If such a tribunal decides that a judge has seriously compromised the judiciary through unethical or illegal acts, it may remove him from office. Such removals have been most frequent in the two states with the longest experience with this type of tribunal—California and New York.[55] Indeed, simply bringing charges or threatening to do so may lead to the judge's resignation. Such removal proceedings, however, do not involve a very broad cross-section of the political arena. Only judges and a segment of the legal profession are involved. Neither party organizations nor significant elements of the general public have any role in the removal of errant judges.

[52] Jacob, "Judicial Insulation."
[53] *State Court Systems* (Lexington, Kentucky: Council of State Governments, 1970), Table VII.
[54] Ibid., Table IX.
[55] For the California experience, see Cook, *The Judicial Process in California*, pp. 55–57.

Moreover, the grounds for removal are quite narrow. Judges may be removed only for misconduct. They cannot be removed by tribunals because they do not work hard enough, are incompetent, are often reversed by appellate courts, espouse unpopular political or judicial philosophies, or quarrel with other officials in the city. Judges enjoy much greater job security than most public officials.

CONCLUSION

Court personnel reflect quite different characteristics than might be expected from the flow of cases into the courts. The commercial interests—who are most advantaged by the gatekeepers of the courts—are not heavily represented in official judicial positions. Rather, middle-income groups—which have most difficulty in using civil courts but who perhaps have most to fear from rampant crime—are most fully represented on the bench and in public prosecutors' and defenders' offices.

These characteristics of the men who staff the courts is an outcome of the incentives, the workload, and the informal qualifications posed by the selection procedures used to fill the various positions. If there is an upper-middle-class bias in the courts, it is not the *direct* result of selecting men with this bias to fill courtroom positions. Since many prosecutors, defenders, and judges come from relatively modest backgrounds, one might expect more sympathetic understanding of the poor and not-quite poor in the courts. A few judges see their role in such terms. George W. Crockett, a black judge in Detroit, stated his perception in these terms:

> Now a black judge has another role to perform. We who are products of the American common law are always extolling the virtue of a common law system and its ability to adapt to the growing needs of the people. In the past, white judges have really made the common law adaptable to what they conceive to be the desires of the American people. We black judges have to take a page from that book. If the common law is so adaptable, let's get down to books and find the remedies, and apply them to the old evils that have plagued the poor and the underprivileged in our society for so long. The answers are there. The special role of the black judge is to see what justice requires and then go to the books and get the remedies to apply to it. Most people assume that the law is something that is clear cut, it's written out, it's black and white; it's not so. Most of the law is a matter of discretion. What is discretion? Discretion is whatever the judge thinks it is as long as he can give a sound reason for it. A judge is a product of his own experiences, of his own history, of the people from whom he came. So a black judge's exercise of discretion is not going to be necessarily the same as that of a white judge. But as long

as it is reason, and the law made by precedent established by white people, that discretion stands. That's the big record that is available.[56]

But for most officials, background characteristics do not determine attitudes. The prestige of the courts helps many prosecutors and judges look to the upper-middle class as its reference group. Although not a part of the upper crust of the legal profession in big cities, they enjoy attention and flattery from them. Many look forward to where they would like their children to be rather than backward to where they spent their own childhoods. Consequently, the distribution of outcomes generated by trial courts is usually not entirely determined by the social backgrounds of official decision-makers. Their backgrounds are only one ingredient in a complex process.

[56] George W. Crockett, "The Role of the Black Judge," *Journal of Public Law*, XX (1971), 398–99. Reprinted by permission of the publisher.

five

THE STRUCTURE
OF
URBAN COURTS

Justice is administered in many settings. As we have already indicated, the police make many decisions that affect the distribution of justice; most police actions occur on the street and they probably affect more citizens than decisions made in any other setting. Attorneys do most of their work in their offices, but they also conduct many negotiations in courthouse hallways. City agencies like the building department, the housing authority, and the contracts and supply department play significant roles in mediating disputes between citizens or settling disputes between individual citizens and public agencies.

The most important *institutional* setting for the administration of justice, however, is the court. Courts provide the stage for prosecutors, attorneys, judges, and other participants to play their roles in the administration of justice. All significant acts do not occur in court, but the characteristics of court structure affect both in-court and out-of-court decision-making. All but the smallest towns have several courts; large cities have many. These courts vary in numerous ways and often provide a choice of forum for litigants. The choice not only involves legal technicalities but also entails expectations about likely responsiveness to particular kinds of claims.

UNDERLYING ORGANIZATIONAL CHARACTERISTICS

Federalism

The fact that the United States is organized as a federal political system has immediate importance to the organization of courts. The federal constitution authorized Congress to establish whatever courts it deemed necessary, but the constitution did not give the federal government exclusive control over the administration of justice. The First Congress established district courts and circuit courts to hear trials involving federal matters whereas the Supreme Court became the final appellate court. Most legal matters, however, were left to the already existing state courts. Thus from the very birth of the nation, two coordinate court systems developed.

In 1970, the federal government had ninety-three district courts which serve as general trial courts for most cases involving federal law.[1] These courts handle criminal as well as civil cases. All the courts are located in major urban centers, although many relatively large cities do not have a full-time federal court in their midst.

Although federal law is a relatively small segment of the total legal code in the United States, a growing variety of conflicts may be brought to the federal courts. When a conflict involves citizens of two states and at least $10,000, it may be brought to a federal court, although it may also be taken to the state courts. Claims arising from federal laws—such as the Civil Rights Acts or the Anti-Trust Acts must be brought to federal court. An increasing number of crimes have also been made part of federal jurisdiction by new legislation and by interpreting broadly the use of interstate commerce in carrying out a crime or dispensing of its fruits. Thus, most major fraud cases and instances of official corruption can be prosecuted under one federal law or another, although state laws also permit prosecution in local courts.

The federal courts possess their own structure of appeals courts. The United States is divided into eleven regions, each one having a Court of Appeals. If an appeal is filed,[2] it must usually be brought to the appropriate Court of Appeals.[3] Somewhat more than one-third of the cases appealed to

[1] Administrative Office of the United States Courts, *Annual Report, 1970* (Washington: Government Printing Office, 1970), p. 142.

[2] Appeals are filed for about two-thirds of all cases adjudicated by trials; see data in The American Almanac for 1972 (New York: Grosset and Dunlap, Inc., 1972), 151.

[3] Cases heard by special three-judge courts are appealed directly to the U.S. Supreme

the Courts of Appeal are appealed further to the U. S. Supreme Court. Most cities having a population of over 50,000 also have a set of state courts which operate at the side of the federal courts but are organizationally independent of them. Although federal courts usually pay more handsome salaries, state courts are not hierarchically "inferior" to the federal district courts. The state courts handle some of the same disputes as federal courts but generally receive a larger share of the minor litigation. In most locales, the state courts have less prestige than the federal court. Lawyers often think that federal judges are more expert,[4] although in disputes embroiling local values, many litigants think that local courts are more responsive to local norms.[5]

State law determines the organization of local courts. Each state has its own traditional court organization, so that the names of courts, their relationship to one another, and the rules governing their operation vary considerably. In most states, courts share the same organizational characteristics in big cities, small towns, and tiny county seats. Accommodation to urban problems is overlaid on the basic court structure that governs the judiciary for the entire state.

Most large cities have many different courts whose names give little hint of their functions. In most places, no one except lawyers knows where to take a particular case.[6] For instance, Connecticut cities, during the 1960's had a Circuit Court, Court of Common Pleas, Superior Court, Probate Court, and Juvenile Court. The Circuit Court heard the most petty cases; the Court of Common Pleas heard somewhat more important cases; and the Superior Court decided civil cases involving large sums of money and serious criminal matters; the Probate Court handled the administration of estates; and the Juvenile Court heard quasi-criminal charges against juveniles.[7] Baltimore, Maryland, by contrast, had a People's Court for minor cases, a Circuit Court for serious cases, an Orphan's Court for estates, and a Juvenile Court.[8] Milwaukee, Wisconsin,

---

Court. Such cases are rare. For a brief discussion of these courts see Herbert Jacob, *Justice in America*, 2nd ed. (Boston: Little, Brown and Co., 1972), p. 150.

[4] Marvin R. Summers, "Analysis of Factors that Influence Choice of Forum in Diversity Cases," *Iowa Law Review*, XLVII (1962), 937.

[5] This was particularly evident in civil rights cases initiated in the South during the 1950's; see Jack W. Peltason, *Fifty-eight Lonely Men*, 2nd ed. (Champaign: University of Illinois Press, 1971).

[6] An early description of this confusion is provided by Albert Lepawsky, *The Judicial System of Metropolitan Chicago* (Chicago: University of Chicago Press, 1932).

[7] I. Ridgeway Davis, David Mars and Fred Kort, *Administration of Justice in Connecticut* (Storrs, Connecticut: Institute of Public Service, University of Connecticut, 1963).

[8] Elbert M. Byrd, Jr., *The Judicial Process in Maryland* (College Park, Md.: University of Maryland Bureau of Governmental Research, 1961).

had a County Court and a Municipal Court for minor cases plus a Circuit Court for major ones. Juvenile matters and estates were handled by segments of the Circuit Court.[9] Thus, no single description includes the entire nation, nor can we identify general tendencies for particular kinds of cities. Court structure is almost entirely a matter of state legislation and tradition.

The state courts function within the context of their own set of appeals courts and procedural rules which are promulgated by appellate courts or state legislatures. Most states have an intermediate appellate court which either sits in regional divisions or is located at the state capital. Most appeals first go to this intermediate court before moving to the state supreme court. The state supreme court is the final arbiter of state law, although some cases, because they involve federal questions, may be taken to the U. S. Supreme Court. Although the full set of appeals is available on equal grounds to all litigants, relatively few take their case to an appeals court, and even fewer move beyond the first appeal to review by a supreme court.

The implications of this dual legal system and court structure are manifold. The jurisdiction of federal courts often responds to different political demands. In some instances, groups which are helpless minorities in their city seek through Congressional action to enlarge the jurisdiction of federal courts. This effort permits them to obtain relief for their problems in federal courts which they cannot secure in the state and local political system. For instance, federal civil rights statutes authorize federal courts to provide relief against public discrimination and to punish persons who interfere with exercise of civil rights. In many cities, such actions could not be otained from state courts. In other instances, federal courts are given jurisdiction because an interest group wishes to obtain more uniform regulation of behavior than is likely when local courts interpret the statutes of fifty states. This objective was the concern of business interests in seeking inclusion of the commerce clause in the federal constitution. Subsequently, the commerce clause has been used by business interests to obtain from Congress more uniform standards of doing business across the country and by reform groups to achieve national regulation of what they consider commercial abuses. Because the groups which control the national legislative process in Congress are seldom the same as the ones that control legislation in the state capitals, state and federal laws often overlap. Both federal and state courts often have jurisdiction over the same disputes in a city.

The inverse side of the federal courts' responsiveness to different

[9] Wisconsin Judicial Council, *1969 Judicial Statistics*, mimeo.

groups is that governing elites in cities find the presence of federal courts a constant threat of external interference in their affairs. Since the federal courts' jurisdiction and personnel are subject to less direct influence from local elites, the danger of unwanted meddling is somewhat greater. For instance, after local compromises have been hammered out on school busing or environmental control, a federal court suit may upset the arrangements.

Hierarchical Controls

The second constant characteristic of American courts is that they operate under loose or non-existent hierarchical controls. State supreme courts and the U. S. Supreme Court are supreme in the sense that they hear appeals from other courts and sometimes formulate rules of procedures for lower courts. But they do not control the assignment of personnel, the formulation of the budget, or the distribution of supplies and facilities among the courts or the flow of cases through each tribunal. These matters are left almost entirely to individual judges or to court systems in a particular locale.

In most cities, however, the state courts and the federal district court have their own set of administrative controls. Each has a presiding judge who often controls the assignment of judges to particular courtrooms, supervises the flow of cases, administers local rules of procedure, and negotiates with city and county officials for their operating budget and physical facilities. In the federal courts, the chief judge is selected by seniority; he is the most senior of the judges who has not reached the age of seventy; he serves until he becomes seventy years old. In local courts, presiding judges are usually elected by the other judges of the court. Where several levels of courts exist in the city, each has its own administrative judge, and they operate independently of each other.

The powers of an administrative judge may be considerable. Although he cannot remove a judge from his court, he may give him an undesirable assignment—to an outlying courtroom, to a badly equipped courtroom, or to one that handles obnoxious cases such as Narcotics Court. Administrative judges also routinely shift other judges from one court to another in response to shifts in the workload because the administrative judges are responsible for insuring optimal disposition of cases. They also have extra influence over the appointment of auxiliary court personnel such as bailiffs, clerks, and other functionaries. Since these posts constitute a considerable portion of the patronage available in most cities, administrative judges hold a strategic position in the distribution of this resource. In addition, chief judges often have special responsibilities and powers to deal with emergencies.[10] During the riots which occurred in many cities between 1965 and 1968, many city courts operated under special procedures ordered by the chief judges. For instance, the amount of bail required for the release of prisoners was subject to extraordinary rules imposed by the chief judges in Detroit and in Chicago; rules permitting lawyers to represent clients were also altered during the riots.

Specialization

A considerable degree of differentiation exists in state and local courts. Almost all urban trial courts differ along three dimensions. The first dimension concerns the seriousness of the case as measured by the amount of money involved in civil litigation and the possible punishment in criminal cases. Separate courts hear "minor" and "major" cases, except that the U. S. District Court hears all cases involving federal law, but these cases involve relatively few "minor" matters. Among the local courts, the ones that specialize in minor matters also often decide the preliminary stages (such as bail setting or preliminary hearings) of "major" criminal cases.[11] The exact division among courts is different in each state and often within a city, several courts have overlapping jurisdiction.

The second dimension is a functional one. In most cities certain kinds of conflict are singled out for special treatment. The U. S. District Court has one special office for handling bankruptcy matters and a specially appointed official—the Referee in Bankruptcy—disposes of most bankruptcy petitions. A second special official, the federal magistrate, handles all preliminary matters in federal criminal cases. The local courts usually have special divisions or entirely separate courts for probating wills, hearing divorce cases, handling criminal charges involving juveniles, and disposing of traffic offenses. In addition, less formalized specialization may exist, with particular courtrooms handling mostly prostitution cases, other courtrooms designated for narcotics offenses, and still others for assaults involving husbands and wives. Specialization is usually greater in large metropolitan centers than in small cities because the volume of cases does not justify the existence of specialized courtrooms in small urban centers.

---

[10] "Criminal Justice in Extremis: Administration of Justice During the April 1968 Chicago Disorder," *University of Chicago Law Review*, XXXVI (1969), 464–65, 528–30; "Administration of Justice in the Wake of the Detroit Civil Disorder of July, 1967," *University of Michigan Law Review*, LXVI (1968), 1544.

[11] In federal court, such matters are handled by a federal magistrate who is an officer of the court.

The third dimension of differentiation is between criminal and civil cases. Criminal cases are ones in which an offense is alleged which the government is willing to prosecute in the place of the person who was harmed; it is a violation of the laws of the community, and the remedy that the courts authorize is punishment. Civil cases are disputes between private parties or between citizens and their government. The government does not usually take the place of the private litigant in pressing the case; the remedies are generally not punitive but compensatory or rehabilitative. For instance, in a civil action arising from an automobile accident, the driver at fault is made to pay for the damages his carelessness caused, but he is not jailed because of his carelessness.[12]

There are numerous overlaps between these distinctions. A person may be forced to compensate his victim in a criminal case whereas a civil case may lead to the assessment of punitive as well as compensatory damages. However, the rules governing civil and criminal proceedings still have many differences between them. The burden of proof in criminal cases is beyond a reasonable doubt whereas in civil cases it is only the preponderance of the evidence. The right to a jury trial is much more limited in civil cases; the juries may be smaller and decide by a non-unanimous vote in civil cases in many states.[13] Defense and plaintiff exchange much more information in civil suits than do defense and prosecution in criminal cases. The rules for introducing evidence and for deciding jurisdiction often differ considerably.

An important consequence of dividing courts into civil and criminal divisions is that the clientele of the two courtrooms are quite different. Criminal courts are crowded with the poor, the dirty, the near-untouchables of American society. Civil courts are populated by well-dressed clients, mostly businessmen, who occupy positions of prestige and status in the society. Although conflict is often sharp in both kinds of courtroom, civil courts are less unpleasant than those which handle criminal cases.

In most cities, the two kinds of cases are regularly handled by distinct courts. Personnel may shift from one court to another on a regular rotation, or their duties may be completely separate. But at least for some time, one set of officials specializes in criminal deviance whereas another set specializes in private disputes. The former are in the courtrooms which

---

12 An additional distinction is between cases that arise in law and ones that arise in equity. This distinction rests on the historical power of courts to grant some remedies out of a concern for equity that the law did not explicitly provide. Divorces were once equity cases and are still sometimes considered as such even though divorce is now the subject of an extensive body of statutory law. Injunctions are also considered as equitable remedies according to that legal tradition. Equity cases are now generally handled by civil courts, much like other civil cases.

13 However, several states also permit non-unanimous jury verdicts in criminal cases.

the poor see mostly; the latter are those which better-placed citizens see. The former are often undisciplined and chaotic; the latter are calm, well disciplined, smooth operations.

Specialization and differentiation may be manifested in several ways. In some cities, the courts are specialized with distinct rules for each kind of proceeding. This practice is most often the case in juvenile courts, which operate under their own rules of procedure and which dispense a somewhat different set of sanctions than adult courts. Small claims courts also often have their own sets of procedural rules. Although the statutory base for such differentiation is often missing in the case of other courts, it may exist on an ad hoc basis. For instance, in Wisconsin the author found the clerk of court acting as judge in wage garnishment cases in place of the small claims judge in several cities.[14]

Another form of differentiation is one in which most of the courts operate under uniform procedures, but the judges are specialized. This practice means a particular judge—for instance, one elected as a circuit court judge—sits for years on the juvenile division of the court and becomes an expert in handling juvenile cases.

Specialization is a response both to particularistic pressures for reform or special treatment and to work loads in large cities. Juvenile courts represent specialization that developed in response to interest group pleading. The groups were social reformers who felt that the general courts did not treat juveniles appropriately.[15] The criminal courts were thought to criminalize young boys and girls who had barely begun a criminal career.[16] By segregating youngsters from adult courts, reformers felt that individualized treatment could be given and children saved from lifelong criminality. The new courts not only separated children from adults but also applied civil procedures to criminal matters; this approach led to the application of different standards of proof and different kinds of punishment for violations of the criminal code. In juvenile courts, children could be placed under state supervision without proof that they had committed a specific criminal act. They could not obtain jury trials. Lawyers were discouraged from interfering in juvenile proceedings because it was felt that their overemphasis on legal technicalities would stand in the way of providing the best possible treatment for the child. Finally, a record of delinquency was not to be equivalent to a criminal conviction

---

[14] Herbert Jacob, Debtors in Court (Chicago: Rand McNally & Co., 1969), pp. 99–100.

[15] Anthony M. Platt, The Child Savers: The Invention of Delinquency (Chicago: University of Chicago Press, 1969), especially pp. 101–36.

[16] Margaret K. Rosenheim. "Perennial Problems in the Juvenile Court," in Justice for the Child, ed. Margaret K. Rosenheim (New York: The Free Press, 1962), pp. 1–12; also Platt, The Child Savers.

and, therefore, it was hoped, would not stigmatize the child when he became an adult.

Most states adopted some form of the juvenile court for their urban areas. In some cities, the court is simply a part-time assignment for one of the ordinary judges, and every judge takes his turn in juvenile court. In other cities, particular judges are designated as juvenile judges and retain this assignment for years at a time. Some of these juvenile judges seek to equip themselves to deal with children by extra study of child psychology and by developing close relations with child welfare agencies and institutions.

The small claims court was also the product of a reform movement.[17] Champions of the common man sought this court in order to make judicial remedies available to people who could not afford an attorney, high fees, and a long wait in order to settle a relatively small claim. The courts were originally intended for claims not exceeding $25 or $50, although now their limits have been increased to as much as $500. Again, the specialization was based on the characteristics of the clientele group. The small claims court was also marked by special procedures. The judicial process was simplified so that any literate person could fill out the required forms and handle his own case before the judge. No juries were permitted and trials generally amounted to hearing only the complainant, defendant, and a handful of witnesses. Judges made their decisions immediately after hearing the case so that in the course of an hour, the dispute was resolved, unless an appeal was made to a higher court, something that happened rarely. The court often sat at night in order to permit working people to bring their case without losing a day's work.

Traffic court is an instance of specialization in response to the volume of cases. Every large city generates a huge volume of parking tickets and traffic summonses. These cases involve a cross-section of the population. The violation of traffic regulations is not considered criminal behavior by most of the public and generally involves the imposition of standard fines. Consequently, every city has developed alternative procedures. For the lesser offenses, the "court" is a postal operation with motorists mailing their fine to the court. More serious offenses require personal attendance in court before a judge. If the driver pleads guilty, a standard fine is assessed that can be paid on the spot; if he pleads innocent, a hearing is held later that day or on another day when he and the arresting policemen testify. Although attorneys are often present to represent the defendant, the hearings proceed with great rapidity and informality.

Traffic court, like juvenile court, is sometimes a separate facility and

---

[17] James Willard Hurst, The Growth of American Law (Boston: Little, Brown and Co., 1950), pp. 159–63.

sometimes simply a branch of another court with a quasi-permanent judge assigned to hear only these matters. As with juvenile judges, there is a sufficient degree of permanency in these assignments to sustain a national association of traffic judges.

The degree of specialization in the courts, however, is surprisingly low when compared to medicine, business, or academic disciplines. In part, this is true because the bar is not specialized. Mostly it is because the legal tradition of generalized courts which handle all judicial business is so strong that most special interest groups have been unable to obtain particular tribunals for their cases.

Areal Organization

The areal organization of courts is also significant for understanding the operation of the judiciary in American cities. Most courts operating in American cities serve more than the city; they also serve a large portion of suburbia; and in the case of federal district courts, they serve much of the rural hinterland of the city. However, when metropolitan areas spill over state lines, entirely separate state and federal courts operate on the two sides of the boundaries.

The areal jurisdiction of a court is important in many ways. It often determines whether a court has the right to hear a particular complaint. Complex rules allocate disputes to courts according to where an infraction took place and where the litigants reside. Since each local court is to some degree an independent entity and because the substantive law may vary from city to city and from state to state, the place where a suit is filed and the procedures that are applied there may significantly affect the outcome of the suit.

The location of a court also influences its responsiveness to political interests. Rural judges are less likely to understand or to empathize with urban problems; they may seek to apply the norms of a small town upon the residents of a large city in such matters as traffic infractions, violation of blue laws which prohibit certain businesses from operating on Sundays, liquor and drug offenses, gambling and vice. Judges unfamiliar with a particular court system may not be a party to the informal understandings that lubricate the ongoing transactions between prosecutor and defendant and between attorneys and judges; their rulings are likely to appear unpredictable and to upset the equilibrium of out-of-court bargaining. The areal organization of the courts reduces the likelihood of such incidents. In most states, the county is the fundamental judicial district; courts are located in county seats, and the courts in one county are substantially independent of those in another. This organization means that the judges usually come from the county which they serve;

they rarely sit on other courts, and outsiders rarely sit on their court. The lawyers and clients served by a county's court are mostly residents of the county. The other officials working in the court are locals. Every element of court organization reinforces the local character of the court and minimizes the influence of outsiders. The parochial character of courts is so strong that business firms who need to use a court outside their home office often retain a local lawyer rather than sending one from their headquarters staff because local lawyers know the essential local customs and have the required local connections to optimize the client's chances of success.

Since all cities and many metropolitan areas are contained within a single county, they are often served by a single set of courts. In addition to the county courts, most cities also have municipal courts whose jurisdiction extends only to the city's boundaries. These courts are successors to the rural justice of the peace and generally handle relatively minor criminal and civil disputes. They hear traffic cases, offenses against local ordinances, misdemeanors, hold preliminary hearings for felonies, and decide suits involving small amounts of money (generally not exceeding $1,000). Municipal courts also enforce local ordinances. Both municipal courts and county courts are partially insulated from the influence of outsiders. Outsiders in the state legislature make the most of laws that these courts must enforce; outsiders may come to these courts as litigants. But the character of these courts as *local* courts remains undisputed.

The areal structure of courts does not insure every population group equal influence over the courts. Indeed, the areal structure denies such influence to many groups. One important set of citizens with reduced influence are suburbanites. Courts are almost always located in the central city. Where the central city dominates elections in the county, central-city voters and political organizations are likely to have more influence in the election of court personnel. The case load is also likely to be made up mostly of inner-city disputes, and the norms developed in resolving them are likely to be applied to suburban cases as well. Because this fact presents a real problem, some metropolitan areas have been subdivided into central city and suburban districts, providing suburbanites with influence over the courts which have jurisdiction over their disputes.[18] In Boston, for instance, judges are appointed by the governor. For misdemeanors, they serve in relatively small districts whose populations are more homogeneous than that of the entire state or of the metropolitan areas. More than half the defendants in the central-city

---

[18] For Chicago, see Wesley G. Skogan, "Party and Constituency in Political Recruitment: The Case of the Judiciary in Cook County," Illinois, Ph. D. dissertation, Northwestern University, 1971.

district courts are black; the central city is also where most blacks live. In the suburban courts, the proportion of black residents and defendants decreases. Central-city defendants receive much harsher treatment in these circumstances than suburbanites. Far fewer defendants are released on personal recognizance bail in the central-city courts than in the suburbs; fewer are found "not guilty"; more of those convicted are sent to jail.[19] In other suburban areas, police show a greater reluctance to arrest and charge because their constituents will be subjected to the same treatment as central-city offenders. Police discretion thus compensates for lack of direct influence over court disposition of cases.

Judicial districts are generally not so small that particular ethnic or occupational groups achieve proportional representation on the local courts. Court districts are not wards and precincts. Consequently, minority groups concentrated in small portions of the city are not likely to win proportional representation on the bench and do not have courts that serve them exclusively. Blacks in central cities rarely have as many judges on the bench as their population would warrant; they almost never have courts that serve black communities exclusively. The same is true of other ethnic minorities that live in district neighborhoods.

CONSTANCY AND CHANGE IN COURT STRUCTURES

The significance of court structure for litigants and for other participants in the political arena becomes most evident in times of stress, when open conflict erupts over plans to change structure. Such struggles occur with regularity as they do with all government agencies because attempts are made to adapt existing court structures to new social conditions.

The most important observation about change in court structure is that extraordinarily little of it has occurred in the last century. While the nation has quintupled its population and become predominantly urban rather than rural, while the economy has become nationwide rather than regional, while electricity and electronics have replaced steam and horsepower, while blacks have become free men in actuality as well as myth, and while millions of white ethnics have poured into the United States to undermine the predominance of Anglo-Saxon Protestants, the courts have changed only in minor details. This lack of change reflects the strength of the legal tradition and legal culture which have successfully

---

[19] Stephen R. Bing and S. Stephen Rosenfeld, *The Quality of Justice in the Lower Criminal Courts of Metropolitan Boston* (Boston: Lawyers Committee for Civil Rights Under Law, 1970), pp. 68, 86.

resisted change and have accommodated innovation in ways that avoid external alterations. For instance, the criminal prosecution process has become fundamentally different through the development of plea bargaining over the past century and a half, but this change has happened so slowly and so subtly that no historian has recorded it, and few structural innovations give evidence of it. Many other subtle changes have occurred that bypass outmoded structures or use them in new ways. Thus, the credit-card economy with widespread consumer indebtedness has developed since World War II without changes in the courts; personal injury litigation has become the most common form of civil action because of the prevalence of automobile injuries, but the courts have not changed to adapt themselves to the flow of this litigation.

The resilience of court structure and the strength of opponents to change are exposed in studies of attempts at judicial reform.[20] These studies show that the principal opponents of reform are lawyers, officials of the court system, interests that fear less favorable treatment under changed structures, and city politicos entrenched in the existing system.

Large numbers of attorneys [21] oppose alterations of court structure because such changes unsettle their work routines and the network of contacts which facilitate negotiations and settlements. In opposing changes, attorneys act not only from self-interest but also as representatives of particular clients who may suffer reverses under different structures. The maze of courts and alternative forums that typifies most unreformed city court structures, for instance, benefits the well-represented client (e.g., a consumer finance company) at the cost of the often unrepresented individual defendant. For in addition to justifying a considerable fee because the attorney is able to steer his client through the maze, the confusing court structure allows him to choose the most advantageous forum, the one in which the defendant is least likely to appear or the one before which the defendant has the most difficulty making an adequate defense. For instance, until recently, New York city courts permitted creditors to file suits against delinquent debtors in courts that were miles away from where the debtors lived or from where the transaction took place. A hapless debtor in Harlem thus got a notice to appear in a court in Westchester County; [22] three-quarters of the defend-

---

[20] Gilbert Y. Steiner and Samuel K. Gove, *Legislative Politics in Illinois* (Champaign: University of Illinois Press, 1960), pp. 165–98; Kermit W. Smith, "The Politics of Judicial Reform in New Jersey," Ph. D. dissertation, Princeton University, 1964; Donald P. Kommers, "Judicial Politics in Wisconsin: A Case Study in Court Reorganization," unpublished paper, 1965.

[21] However, some attorneys—notably ones who do not have large trial practices but who are influential in bar associations—support judicial reform.

[22] David Caplovitz, *Debtors in Default* (New York: Columbia University Bureau of Applied Social Research, 1971), Chapter 11, p. 39.

ants in creditor suits discovered in a recent study did not live in the borough in which the suits were filed.[23] The reformer—seeking efficiency and minimized costs—views such anomalies as wasteful and unjust. Creditors find them advantageous. Although debate over reform often disguises the direct conflict of interest that we have just described, this conflict motivates many of the opponents of reform.

This conflict is equally explicit in the actions of judges who oppose reform. Many court reforms have sought (with considerable success in recent years) to abolish the post of Justice of the Peace, an elected judge who hears the most trivial cases and ordinance violations. Justices of the Peace often do not hold law degrees; their post is a sinecure from which the incumbent obtains an income based on a percentage of the fines and fees that he collects. Although most prevalent in rural areas, it still exists in some small cities. Because Justices of the Peace are elected officials and win their post in return for helping other candidates during campaigns, they are well connected with legislators and county officials. When reformers have sought to abolish their posts, the Justices of the Peace have rallied these allies to help ward off reform. In many instances, they have succeeded wholly; in others, they won inclusion of incumbents into a new magistracy system which incorporated all incumbent justices into a new magistrate's post but provided that future magistrates would have to have legal training (e.g., Missouri). Justices of the Peace, however, are not the only judicial opponents of reform. In Wisconsin, for instance, circuit court judges blocked reform of trial courts until they were reassured that their greater prestige would not be diluted by incorporation with the county courts.[24]

City politicos often oppose reform. The courts provide a major source of patronage, and they resist changes that may cause them to lose that patronage through the introduction of a merit system or through structural alterations that make the courts less dependent on other local officials. In Illinois, for instance, the Democratic machine in Cook County was willing to accept merit re-election of incumbent judges but not their initial selection by a commission of outsiders; initial-selection judges remains the prerogative of the slate-makers, the caucus of influential party activists. In Milwaukee, where no strong political machine has recently held power, city politicos nevertheless resisted state-wide judicial reform because it threatened to upset the specialized court system that had developed through years of particular legislation and local custom. Since Milwaukee is the only really large metropolitan area in the state, its officials feared that outstate legislators and judges would not

---

[23] Caplovitz, *Debtors in Default*, Chapter 11, p. 40.
[24] Donald P. Kommers, "The Development and Organization of the Wisconsin Court System," Ph. D. dissertation, University of Wisconsin, 1963, pp. 542–635.

appreciate the unusual circumstances governing judicial business in a metropolis. The opposition of city officials to state-wide judicial reform reflects a more general opposition to interference by outsiders in city affairs. Because most courts are state agencies in the sense that they are authorized and molded by state constitutions and state law, court reform has often been a state-wide movement. The earlier exceptions that were granted to cities (such as their establishment of unified municipal courts) are now threatened by a new generation of reformers who seek to impose identical structures on the state as a whole. Adaptation to peculiar conditions of each locality and urban area thus becomes more difficult.

Court reform rarely becomes an issue of wide public controversy, even though resistance to it may be stubborn. The reason is that the benefits of reform are often diffuse rather than manifestly advantageous to particular groups. Hence court reform at best commands broad but shallow public approval. Few, for instance, oppose efficient courts in the abstract, but few also find judicial efficiency a salient issue. In some cases, reform is proposed to benefit a particular group—such as youthful offenders through the adoption of juvenile courts. The beneficiaries, however, do not possess sufficient resources to promote the reform themselves; hence such a reform is the product of efforts by surrogates who claim to speak in behalf of the beneficiaries of reform. Such reform by surrogates rather than under the direction of the beneficiaries themselves is less likely to bestow planned benefits upon the intended objects of reform because the surrogates rarely have a complete understanding of the problems facing the objects of their beneficence and because the beneficiaries are unable to monitor the execution of reform proposal once the interest of its patrons is gone. Indeed, that has been the result of the juvenile court movement. Although reformers had hopes that juveniles would be treated less harshly than adult criminals, the treatment of young offenders has often been more severe.[25] Juveniles may be imprisoned for longer periods than adults for similar offenses; the conditions of their imprisonment are often worse than those for adults. However, the beneficiaries of the reform could not organize to achieve better conditions themselves. Juvenile delinquents form a group in the sense that sociologists, penologists and other outside observers treat them as an aggregate. Many do not, however, associate with each other on the basis of their age and delinquency until they are imprisoned; they lack all other associational resources as well. If reform is to take place with respect to juvenile courts, it must be undertaken by surrogates and is unlikely to represent the interests of its beneficiaries.

[25] H. Warren Dunham, "The Juvenile Court: Contradictory Orientations in Processing Offenders," Law and Contemporary Problems, XXIII (1958), 512–25; Ketcham, "The Unfulfilled Promise."

Such is the case of many court reforms. Potential users are rarely organized into associational groups; they frequently are low-status, low-income, low-influence persons who cannot successfully negotiate the political process in their own behalf. The surrogates who speak for them are not representatives in the sense that the beneficiaries have authorized them to act as their representatives. Moreover, the knowledge that surrogates have of the preferences of the powerless is often systematically biased by the values of the surrogates themselves. Surrogate reformers are interested in reform because they want to "uplift" and to "reform" the downtrodden as well as to alter the institutions that process them. Consequently, court reforms which are intended to benefit non-influential residents of a city often go astray and are much less beneficial than intended.

The structure of city courts usually does not reflect transient political majorities. Well-endowed litigants can often adapt existing court structures to their purposes without formal changes that require legislative or constitutional reform. Other litigants may find themselves substantially disadvantaged by structures which do not easily accommodate the frictions generated by modern urban life.

six

THE DISPOSITION
OF
CRIMINAL CASES

How criminals are convicted is what most of the public associates with urban courts. It has particular symbolic and material importance to the public, since people derive some of their feelings of safety and well-being from the assumption that the courts will dispense speedy and appropriate treatment to criminal defendants. Yet, there is more misunderstanding about the actual processes used by the courts in criminal prosecutions than in most areas of the governmental process.

The process is a complicated one with many stages. At each stage, public officials make discretionary decisions which release suspects or hold them for further processing. As a defendant progresses from one stage to another, his acquittal becomes less likely, although his eventual imprisonment hinges on more than his guilt. Most of the stages involve an appearance before a judge in a public proceeding or an action otherwise nominally visible to the public; nevertheless, most decisions escape public notice because they are so routine, drab, and non-newsworthy.

The formal proceedings begin with the arrest of a suspect. In a few instances, the police may have gone to a judge to obtain a warrant for the arrest; such warrants are routinely granted in most cases. Most arrests, however, are made without a warrant.[1] Since most arrests are made at

---

[1] Wayne R. LaFave, *Arrest: The Decision to Take a Suspect into Custody* (Boston: Little, Brown and Co., 1965), pp. 53–60.

96

night, the police usually may hold a suspect until morning before bringing him before a magistrate, although they must inform him of his constitutional rights. During that time, they usually question him and attempt to obtain a confession. He may, of course, refuse to answer questions or ask to confer with his attorney. He is then brought before a magistrate (a judge of a minor criminal court) and is informed of the charges on which he is being held and again is apprised of his rights. At the same time—or at another hearing on the following day before another judge—bail is set. In most instances, the bail is a monetary guarantee that he will appear in court whenever required for further proceedings. If he has sufficient funds to put up the stipulated bail, he is freed pending trial.[2] In some instances, he is freed upon his promise that he will appear; such a "recognizance" bond is usually made available to defendants without prior criminal records who seem to have firm roots in the community. If the defendant is denied a recognizance bond or if he cannot provide money for a bail bond, he is placed in the local jail until his case is completed—usually three to six months after his arrest if the case involves a serious charge.

In minor cases (misdemeanors with light punishment or offenses against city ordinances), a summary trial may also take place at this stage —almost immediately after the arrest. If the defendant pleads guilty, he is at once given a sentence—often a nominal fine or probation—and sent on his way. If he pleads innocent, the case is usually continued to another date, usually a month or two later. In serious cases (felonies), a preliminary hearing before a judge may be held at which the prosecution displays enough evidence showing probable cause to warrant holding the defendant for trial. In many jurisdictions, the preliminary hearing is waived and is no longer a meaningful element of the disposition process; in others, it plays a very important role. In Chicago, judges and prosecutors use the preliminary hearings to screen out cases which they feel should be handled as minor offenses or should be dismissed entirely.[3] In Los Angeles, the preliminary hearings are also used to record evidence that another judge will later use to decide inocence or guilt and to set the punishment if a conviction results.[4]

[2] In some states—Illinois and Maryland are examples—the defendant must pay 10 per cent of the required bail to the court. If he appears in court, 90 per cent of what he paid is returned to him; the remainder is kept to administer the bail system. In most states, bail is provided by bail bondsmen, comprising a private industry. Bail bondsmen usually also require 10 per cent payment, but it is usually entirely a nonrefundable fee. Moreover, when a bail bondsman does not consider a defendant a good risk, he may refuse to sell him the bond, and the defendant remains in jail.

[3] Donald M. McIntyre, "A Study of Judicial Dominance in the Charging Process," *Journal of Criminal Law, Criminology, and Police Science,* LIX (1968), 463–90.

[4] Kenneth Graham and Leon Letwin, "The Preliminary Hearing in Los Angeles," *UCLA Law Review,* XVIII (1971), 635–757.

After the preliminary hearing, formal accusation is brought against the defendant. In most jurisdictions, the charge is prepared by the prosecutor's office in the form of an information; in others (a minority), the grand jury under the prosecutor's supervision returns an indictment. The information and indictment are formal specification of charges, indicating the laws alleged to have been violated and the acts constituting the violation. The charges in the information or indictment form the basis for further action.

After the charge is drawn by the prosecutor or is voted by a grand jury, the defendant is brought before a judge for his arraignment. At the arraignment, the charges are read to the defendant, and he is asked to plead guilty or not guilty. Many defendants (in some jurisdictions, most of them) plead guilty at this stage and are sentenced.[5] If they plead not guilty, a date for trial is set, but most defendants plead guilty sometime before their trial begins. With very few exceptions, in large cities an overwhelming majority of defendants plead guilty. Only 5–10 per cent plead not guilty and are tried by a judge or jury.

Sentencing defendants who have admitted their guilt or have been convicted at trial is the final step. The sentencing may immediately follow the guilty plea or conviction or it may take place several days later. A judge passes sentence after taking into account information provided by the defense counsel, the prosecutor, and the probation department.[6] Sentences vary considerably between judges and for a single judge over a period of time.[7] Some defendants receive nominal sentences whereas others receive close to the maximum punishment permitted by the law.

These steps comprise the occasions for decision-making by defendants, prosecutors, and judges. Their decision-making may be viewed from the perspective of two quite different models of the legal system. They may be perceived as involving adversary proceedings, or they may be seen as a dispositional process in which negotiation and collaboration, rather than confrontation, are the norm.[8] Although elements of both models exist in most courtroom proceedings, it is essential to understand the assumptions of both models in order to gain an understanding of courtroom encounters.

---

[5] Ted Busch, "Prosecution in Baltimore Compared to the Houston System," The Prosecutor, V (1969), 253–56; Robert S. Fertitta, "Comparative Study of Prosecutors' Offices: Baltimore and Houston, Ibid., 248–52; John J. Meglio, "Comparative Study of the District Attorney's Offices in Los Angeles and Brooklyn," Ibid., 237–41.

[6] Robert O. Dawson, Sentencing (Boston: Little, Brown and Co., 1968).

[7] Albert Somit, Joseph Tanenhaus, and Walter Wilke, "An Aspect of Judicial Sentencing Behavior," University of Pittsburgh Law Review, XXI (1959), 613–20; Frederick J. Gaudet, "Individual Differences in Sentencing Tendencies of Judges," Archives of Psychology, XXXII (1938). For contrary evidence, see Edward Green, Judicial Attitudes in Sentencing (London: Macmillan, 1961).

[8] The classic exposition of the two models is by Herbert L. Packer, The Limits of the Criminal Sanction (Stanford, Calif.: Stanford University Press, 1968).

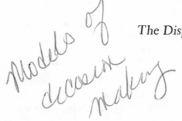

THE ADVERSARY PROCESS

The adversary process is the model that has been accepted as legitimate. Its distinctiveness rests on the assumptions said to motivate its participants. The most important of these assumptions concern the nature of conflict, the objective of the proceedings, and the characteristics of rules that the process requires.

The adversary process operates under the simplifying assumption that conflicts are two-sided or can be presented in the framework of a two-sided dispute. A plaintiff and a defendant present their dispute; in criminal cases, the prosecutor takes the place of a plaintiff. There is little room for other participants who may have an interest in the outcome of the litigation. If others are permitted a voice, it is as friends of the court who intervene on behalf of the plaintiff or defendant. On rare occasions, courts recognize that a case is multi-faceted, or that the various people who compose the plaintiff's or the defendant's side do not really share common interests. But even so, the case, nevertheless, is presented as if it were a two-sided dispute.

In many suits this assumption does not gravely distort reality. In common criminal cases and in the majority of civil conflicts, there are only two disputants—one making a complaint and the other defending against it. But the presumption does confine the presentation of ancillary arguments in cases involving broad social interests, for example, when the outcome will affect a whole class of citizens or when an important principle of law is challenged.[9] In such cases, there are many overlapping interests, and they cannot be compressed into two sides without serious distortion of their views.

The compression of the dispute into two sides is closely related to the adversary process assumption that by airing opposing views, the truth will emerge. Several additional assumptions underlie this view. It is assumed that each side wants to win and will command sufficient resources to make victory possible, if the truth is indeed on its side. It is assumed that finding the truth is the objective, and that courtroom proceedings exist to discover it. It is assumed that having the two sides present their case will expose all pertinent facts and that the rules which govern the trial will allow reasonable men to separate truth from falsehood.

These beliefs rely on a third set of assumptions that characterize the

---

[9] Modifications of the normal adversary process permit the presentation of such interests in "class action" suits at the trial level and through "amicus curiae briefs" at the appellate level. Amicus briefs are more common than class action suits, but neither are part of the normal adversary process.

American adversary process—the central role of due process of law.
Americans are assured by the Fifth and Fourteenth Amendments to the
Constitution that they will not be "deprived of life, liberty, or property
without due process of law. . . ." By judicial interpretation, conditions
which produce a "fair hearing" are incorporated in the constitutional
requirements of due process. The procedures which have been traditionally
thought necessary to produce a fair hearing and "due process" are in part
specified by the Constitution with respect to criminal proceedings.
They include a bar against compulsory self-incrimination, unreasonable
bail, and double jeopardy; the Constitution also guarantees the right to a
speedy and public trial, to an impartial jury, to be informed of the charges
brought against a criminal defendant, to confront witnesses and to compel favorable witnesses to appear in the defendant's behalf. In addition,
courts have ruled that criminal defendants must be provided counsel paid
by the public if they cannot afford their own.[10] Procedural rules permit
both sides to present relevant evidence but require that the evidence must
be first-hand and not based on conjecture or rumor. The rules seek to
establish a certain degree of equality between the two sides by requiring
the government to carry the burden of proof in criminal cases to the point
at which its case has been proved beyond a reasonable doubt; this constitutes the presumption of innocence. An outgrowth of that presumption is the norm that defendants shall be treated *as if* they were innocent.
All parties therefore enter the court as innocent; the presumption of innocence leaves to the court the discovery of the truth and the determination of guilt. The right to a speedy trial in criminal matters not only
prevents a long period during which the defendant suffers from an un-
proved accusation but also guarantees that memories of witnesses will be
fresh when they testify in court; the truth should not be blurred by the
passage of time.

Around these fundamental guarantees, a host of usages have developed which are commonly referred to as "legal technicalities." For instance, there is much current debate about the conditions that distinguish
a legally voluntary confession from an illegal, compelled statement, about
whether a lawyer must be appointed immediately after arrest or when
the defendant appears in court, about whether a trial is still "speedy" if
it occurs six months after arrest.[11] These questions, however, do not
involve mere technicalities. They strike at the core assumptions underlying the adversary process; for if procedures necessary to determine the

[10] The basic decision is Gideon v. Wainwright, 372 U. S. 335 (1963); its coverage now includes all instances where conviction may result in imprisonment: Argersinger
v. Hamlin, 407 U. S. 25 (1972).

[11] These matters were in a state of flux at the time when this book was written.
For current interpretations by the Supreme Court, see recent editions of any constitutional law textbook.

truth are evaded, the truth cannot be discovered by the courtroom proceedings, and the very purpose of a trial will have been subverted.

determine appropriate treatment of defendant

THE DISPOSITIONAL PROCESS

If we view courtroom decision-making as a dispositional process, we approach the proceedings with a very different set of assumptions. We are also alerted to a different set of operating characteristics.

One of the principal assumptions of the dispositional process in criminal cases is that most defendants are guilty, not innocent. The assumption of guilt is based on the observation that the police do not randomly arrest people and bring them to court. Rather, persons who appear in court have attracted the attention of the police because of their suspicious activities and have been screened at the station-house desk or by an assistant prosecutor as appropriate candidates for courtroom disposition. It may not be immediately evident of what offense the prisoner is guilty. For instance, there may be some question about whether he should plead guilty to simple or aggravated assault, to burglary or theft. But no participant in the proceedings—neither judge, prosecutor, defense counsel, nor bailiff—doubts that the defendant is guilty of something.

The goal of the dispositional process, therefore, is not to discover the truth or to separate the innocent from the guilty. Rather, the objective is to determine appropriate treatment for the defendant. Which crime he pleads guilty to (or is convicted of) is significant chiefly because of differences in treatment for particular offenses. Whether he really committed the offense he confesses to is unimportant as long as the treatment that he receives as a result of his conviction is appropriate for him. Consequently, the court proceedings focus as much (and sometimes more) on the characteristics of the defendant, his background, and his future potential than on the particular circumstances which brought him to court. The judge is concerned with who the defendant is rather than what actions he committed.

The principal criterion by which the dispositional process is evaluated is efficiency defined in terms of the number of cases disposed per dollar of resources expended. Hence speedy dispositions are highly valued because they do not strain available resources. Alternative criteria of the adversary process, such as the proportion of defendants found innocent, the degree to which truth is discovered, or the correctness of judicial findings are not pertinent. Indeed, proceedings which found many defendants innocent would be considered highly inefficient; court personnel instead seek high proportions of convictions and guilty pleas as indicators of their efficiency.

The operating characteristics of the dispositional process differ markedly from those of the adversary process. Perhaps the most prominent difference is that defense and prosecuting attorneys are allies rather than adversaries. They share many characteristics and have common interests. Both have an overwhelming concern to maintain a smooth flow of cases and to prevent a breakdown in the decisional process. They are in constant interaction with each other and have a mutual stake in maintaining a cordial relationship. They must be reasonable to each other because they accord each other favors. On one day, the prosecutor becomes indebted to the defense counsel for not driving a harder bargain or for understanding why a particular defendant must be treated more harshly than is normal; on the next, the defense counsel is repaid the debt by more favorable treatment for a client, either in terms of scheduling his case or in terms of the plea that is arranged between the prosecutor and defense counsel. The constant interaction between prosecutor and defense counsel leads to a high level of cooperation between them.[12]

Because the dispositional process is evaluated in efficiency terms, the usual procedure is to obtain a guilty plea from the defendant or to dismiss the charges. Only guilty pleas and dismissed charges enable dispositions to be processed with minimal expense. For instance, a Manhattan prosecutor stated: "Our office keeps eight courtrooms extremely busy trying 5 per cent of the cases. If even 10 per cent of the cases ended in a trial, the system would break down. We can't afford to think very much about anything else." [13] Accordingly, if a defendant insists on a trial, he is often penalized upon being found guilty by the imposition of a harsher penalty. Although the judge usually rationalizes the harsh sentence on the grounds that the defendant caused the state to go to the expense of a trial or has not shown the "remorse" that others presumably display through their guilty plea, the underlying reason for the more severe sentence is that the trials subvert the dispositional process.[14]

Many elements of the dispositional process seek to produce efficient guilty pleas rather than requests for trial. Bail is often set at a relatively high level—higher than probably required to assure appearance at trial. The effect of bail too high for many defendants to meet is that they are remanded to the county jail where they await trial in prison. In 1970,

---

[12] Abraham S. Blumberg, Criminal Justice (Chicago: Quadrangle Books, 1967); Albert W. Alschuler, "The Prosecutor's Role in Plea Bargaining," University of Chicago Law Review, XXXVI (1968), 50–112; Dallen Oaks and Warren Lehman, A Criminal Justice System and the Indigent (Chicago: University of Chicago Press, 1968).

[13] Quoted by Alschuler, "The Prosecutor's Role," p. 55; reprinted by permission of the publisher.

[14] Alschuler, "The Prosecutor's Role," p. 55; also see Martin A. Levin, "Urban Political Systems and Judicial Behavior: The Criminal Courts of Minneapolis and Pittsburgh," Ph. D. dissertation, Harvard University, 1970, Chapter 4, p. 25.

there were more than 160,000 prisoners in local and county jails throughout the United States; 35 per cent were awaiting trial and another 17 per cent had not yet been arraigned.[15] In the jail, prisoners awaiting trial receive no special privileges; they are treated exactly the same way as persons who have been convicted and are serving their time. Although this treatment may appear to be an injustice, it has the effect of inducing guilty pleas because the prisoners have nothing to gain from delay.[16]

In addition, defendants are frequently charged with the commission of multiple crimes and on the most serious charges possible. Defendants, however, are rarely convicted of multiple charges or of the charges that are originally brought against them. Rather, multiple and maximum charges are used to induce guilty pleas. The charges afford the prosecutor room for negotiation by permitting him to offer the defendant a reduced charge or dismissal of ancillary charges in return for his guilty plea.[17]

These characteristics of the dispositional process also have the effect of reinforcing the image of the defendant as a guilty person in the eyes of all participants, including the defendant. Each of these characteristics undermines his self-esteem. He is treated as if he were guilty and as if he were dangerous. Being placed in jail while awaiting trial further degrades him in the eyes of his neighbors, acquaintances and fellow workers, but the procedures are consistent with the presumption of guilt that underlies the dispositional process.

Another striking difference from the adversary proceeding is the absence of formal safeguards for the defendant. Whereas due-process safeguards are rooted in the adversary process, the dispositional process has few procedural restrictions.[18] The most important decisions are made in private—either in the prosecutor's office or in the judge's chambers, where the defendant decides to plead guilty. Other crucial decisions—such as the amount of bail—are made in extraordinarily hurried public proceedings governed by rules of thumb rather than by tailored consideration of the individual defendant's circumstances.[19]

Constraints do exist, however. They grow out of the mutual dependence of the prosecution, defense, and judge. The prosecutor is con-

[15] *Third Annual Report of the Law Enforcement Assistance Administration for Fiscal 1971* (Washington: Government Printing Office, 1972), pp. 93–94.
[16] There are some exceptions to this rule. In Chicago, for instance, the prosecution must go to trial within 120 days or face dismissal of the case unless the defense has asked for a delay. Some defense attorneys gamble on the District Attorney's inefficiency to win the release of their clients after the 120 days have elapsed. Notice, however, that a 120-day jail "sentence" is a relatively severe one for minor offenses.
[17] Alschuler, "The Prosecutor's Role."
[18] *Cf. Santobello v. New York*, 30 L. Ed. 2d 427.
[19] Frederic Suffet, "Bail Setting: A Study of Courtroom Interaction," *Crime and Delinquency*, XII (1966), 318–31.

strained by his need for a high proportion of guilty pleas. To obtain these pleas, he must offer something in consideration for the defendant's cooperation. If his offer is much below "the current rate" or does not offer much improvement over the conditions which the defendant may expect if he has insisted on a trial, the prisoner has no incentive to cooperate and may ask for a trial. The prosecutor, therefore, is constrained to act in such a fashion that defendants are induced to cooperate. Judges must cooperate by imposing harsher sentences on defendants convicted after a trial than on those who plead guilty, by maintaining predictable decision patterns according to which defense and prosecutor can calculate their own actions, and by supporting requests for delay, plea, and sentence made by prosecutors. Rather than being a neutral arbiter as presumed in the adversary process, judges are accomplices in the dispositional process. Another consequence is that where the prosecutor possesses weak evidence or is threatened with a defense that is unusually well prepared and well endowed, he may simply move to dismiss charges rather than commit his meager resources to a serious test of strength. Such an alternative is almost always available to the prosecutor in cases involving obscure crimes and victims. The options are not available for prominent defendants or publicized crimes.[20]

ACTUAL CRIMINAL PROCEEDINGS

Elements of both the adversary and the dispositional process are evident in court proceedings in American cities. Characteristics of the dispositional process dominate in most cities, but important features of the adversary system coexist with those of the dispositional process.

Most misdemeanor and felony cases are disposed of by a guilty plea in American cities.[21] In addition, traffic violations and many other ordinance violations are disposed of by the defendant simply forfeiting his bail in lieu of a fine; few defendants make a court appearance in such cases. The enormous volume of cases that confronts courts compels them to adopt the dispositional rather than adversary process. For instance, in 1969 the courts which handle criminal matters in Milwaukee disposed of

---

[20] Alschuler, "The Prosecutor's Role."

[21] Maureen Mileski, "Courtroom Encounters: An Observation Study of a Lower Criminal Court," Law and Society Review, V (1971), 473–538; Donald M. McIntyre and David Lippman, "Prosecutors and Early Disposition of Felony Cases," American Bar Association Journal, LVI (1970), 1154–59; Dominick Vetri, "Plea Bargaining: Compromises by Prosecutors to Secure Guilty Pleas, University of Pennsylvania Law Review, CXII (1964), 865–908.

11,078 cases; thirty judges handled most of these cases in addition to 95,000 civil cases.[22] If each judge shouldered an equal share of the burden and worked 255 days a year, he would have to dispose of at least thirteen cases every day. The requirements of the adversary process make it impossible to adjudicate thirteen cases per day in trial proceedings. Consequently, Milwaukee judges—like judges in most large cities—disposed of most of their criminal and civil cases through plea bargaining and other elements of the dispositional process.

The plea bargain is the most prominent feature of the dispositional process. It encapsulates the essential characteristics of the process. In most cases, defense counsel are the first to suggest to defendants that they plead guilty to some charge in order to receive quick and favorable treatment from the authorities.[23] But before the defense counsel makes this suggestion, the defendant has already been treated by other court personnel as someone who is probably guilty. This treatment occurs in the bail setting proceeding, at which as many as half of all defendants are remanded to jail because they cannot raise enough money to win their freedom on bail.[24] Treatment based on a presumption of guilt also happens during the interval before the bail proceeding, during which defendants are held in the police lock-up. These prior encounters help to condition defendants to a guilty plea.

The details of the plea are usually arranged by the defense attorney with the prosecutor. Defendants rarely participate in the negotiations except to indicate whether they accept the bargain that has been arranged; they rarely control the nature of the bargain. Judges likewise are usually excluded from the negotiations, although in exceptional cases the bargains may be hammered out in the judge's presence. The purpose of the bargain is to save courtroom and judge time. Although bargaining sessions may be brief (sometimes consisting of no more than an offer and its acceptance), consistent involvement of judges in the bargaining process would defeat the efficiency goals of the dispositional process.

The bargain agreed to between the defense and prosecution is then presented to a judge, usually at the arraignment when the prosecution moves to reduce or to dismiss charges and the defendant pleads guilty. At that time, the judge may inquire whether the defendant really under-

[22] Wisconsin Judicial Council, *1969 Judicial Statistics*, mimeo, p. B-7.
[23] Abraham S. Blumberg, "Lawyers with Convictions," in *The Scales of Justice*, ed. Abraham S. Blumberg (Chicago: Aldine Publishing Co., 1970), pp. 51–68.
[24] Blumberg, "Lawyers with Convictions"; Charles Ares, Anne Rankin, and Herbert Sturz, "The Manhattan Bail Project," *New York University Law Review*, XXXVIII (1963), 67–95; *Proceedings of the National Conference on Bail and Criminal Justice* (Washington, D. C., no publisher, 1965), pp. 151–60.

stands the plea and whether it really is voluntary. That inquiry, however, is usually a formality to make the court records less vulnerable to later attack in an appellate court should the defendant for some reason bring his case to an appeals court (something that rarely happens when a defendant pleads guilty).[25] The defendant has usually been prompted by his attorney to give appropriate answers, even to the question of whether the plea is voluntary and whether it is in response to an offer of special treatment. When, for some reason, the defendant gives inappropriate responses, a brief recess is declared while the defense attorney "confers" with his client and arranges proper answers to the questions which the judge asks.[26]

The case is finally disposed when the judge passes sentence. Deals arranged by the prosecutor are not binding on the judge, but he usually entertains recommendations from the prosecutor. In addition, he may ask for a report on the prisoner from the probation department and may listen to pleas from the defense attorney. The sentencing decision in most states is the judge's alone. However, judges understand plea bargaining and recognize that they must render sentences which lie within the boundaries that the defense and prosecution expect; otherwise, subsequent bargains cannot be made. In addition, the bargain itself establishes constraints on the judge because if the defendant pleads guilty to one charge out of an original four, the maximum possible sentence is reduced. Likewise, if a defendant pleads guilty to a reduced charge, the maximum penalty is likely to be less than for the original charge. Thus, although the prosecutor and defense do not formally obligate the judge to a specific sentence, they arrange affairs so that the defendant is likely to receive a sentence within the range he has been promised.[27]

Such dispositional proceedings run in tandem with proceedings that takes place according to the assumptions and rules of the adversary process. An adversary proceeding is always theoretically available to defendants. If one pleads not guilty, he must be accommodated. Whether an adversary proceeding is held depends on many factors.[28] If the prosecutor is unwilling to make a bargain and the defendant is unwilling to plead guilty to the original charge, a trial must be held. That is the situ-

[25] For official standards, see Standards Relating to Pleas of Guilty (Chicago: American Bar Association, 1968); for actual practices, see Blumberg, Criminal Justice, pp. 39–71.

[26] Blumberg, Criminal Justice.

[27] Unfortunately, no sentencing studies known to the author take into account the prior commitments made by prosecutors. Consequently, the findings of such studies as cited in note 7 above are difficult to interpret.

[28] Alschuler, "The Prosecutor's Role"; Frank W. Miller, Prosecution (Boston: Little, Brown and Co., 1970); Donald J. Newman, Conviction (Boston: Little, Brown and Co., 1966); George F. Cole, "The Decision to Prosecute," Law and Society Review, IV, (1970), pp. 331–44.

ation in many prominent cases where the prosecutor is unwilling to accept a guilty plea to a lesser offense because the crime attracted considerable public notice, and he is afraid of public criticism if he reduces the charges. In addition, however, the private resources of defendants play a considerable role in the choice of proceedings. Defendants who can afford to hire their own attorneys and pay them for a trial may prefer the trial, especially if they believe that the prosecution's case will turn out to be relatively weak. In addition, wealthier defendants who insist on a trial are likely to be free on bail while awaiting trial and to use their request for a trial to delay the proceedings.[29] It is likely that they seek one or more continuances in the hope that the prosecution's case weakens with delay (as witnesses forget events or lose interest in pursuing their complaints). In Chicago there is considerable evidence that adversary proceedings are used in this way and that the continuances granted to private defense attorneys work to the advantage of wealthier defendants.[30] In Pittsburgh, defendants who retain private counsel are much more successful in avoiding harsh judges and finding lenient ones by various judge-shopping techniques.[31] By contrast, indigent defendants represented by assigned counsel or by the public defender are less likely to seek an adversary proceeding, or if they do, to engage in judge-shopping. Many of them are in jail while awaiting disposition of their case; if a trial produces delay, it means that these defendants will stay in jail longer before they know their final fate, and their pre-trial incarceration may not be counted on their final sentence. Furthermore, their defense counsel is not eager to proceed to trial since their resources are quite limited. When an indigent defendant does proceed to trial, he has no guarantee that his attorney will be well prepared because he does not really control his attorney's actions in the same manner as the private defendant, and it is likely that his defense attorney does not have sufficient resources to investigate many cases thoroughly.[32] Consequently, the adversary process is a more viable alternative for the defendant with private resources than for the indigent defendant.

Defendants who demand a trial may seek to have a jury rather than bench trial. Most defendants do not ask for a jury trial, but those who do bring another complicating element into the adversary process. Juries

---

[29] Laura Banfield and C. David Anderson, "Continuances in the Cook County Criminal Courts," *University of Chicago Law Review*, XXXV (1968), 259–316.

[30] Ibid.

[31] R. Stanton Wettick, Jr., "A Study of the Assignment of Judges to Criminal Cases in Alleghany County—The Poor Fare Worse," *Duquesne Law Review*, IX (1970–71), 56–57; Levin, "Urban Political Systems and Judicial Behavior," Chapter 4, pp. 7–9.

[32] Oaks and Lehman, *A Criminal Justice System;* Blumberg, "Lawyers with Convictions."

are composed of laymen who normally have no experience or training in legal affairs. In most cities, jury panels are now usually chosen randomly from voter registration lists, but any particular jury is rarely a representative sample of the population. A twelve-person jury—the largest one used for hearing trials—is too small to be statistically representative. In addition, although the panel from which a jury is chosen may come from a random sample of voter registration lists, these lists themselves under-represent low-income groups because they register to vote less frequently. The process of choosing a particular jury introduces further biases. During the *voir dire* examination of the panel to see whether jurors have prejudices that would prevent them from rendering a fair judgment, the judge and opposing lawyers disqualify jurors who seem to have biases. In controversial cases, selecting a jury takes weeks and systematically excludes some elements of the population. Finally, jury service pays very poorly—usually less than $15 per day. Working men and women who are on an hourly or daily wage that they would lose by serving on the jury cannot afford to serve and often ask to be excused from jury service; salaried white-collar workers and retired persons can more readily afford jury service.[33]

Those defendants who ask for jury trials, therefore, do not quite get a jury of their peers. They obtain a jury of non-professionals, of men and women who are not enmeshed in the mutual obligations of the dispositional process. These jurors make the determination of innocence or guilt and often bring their own values into the deliberations, which has the effect of ameliorating what appears to them harsh provisions of the law. It also introduces an element of uncertainty and unpredictability to the criminal trial.

Trials are not a separate part of the criminal process; they have a spill-over effect on dispositional proceedings. Sentences imposed after a trial set upper limits to the sentences that can realistically be imposed on defendants who plead guilty to similar offenses. Prosecutors must maintain a high record of conviction at trial because, otherwise, defendants who might plead guilty will seek their acquittal at trial. Rulings on evidence at trials also have a spill-over effect on bargaining sessions. Prosecutors and defense attorneys will judge the strength of the evidence by the standards evolved through trials and appeals; if the evidence is weak by these standards, the defense may press for a more lenient disposition or may insist on a trial because of the likelihood of an acquittal. Therefore, even though relatively few trials are held in most cities, they have

[33] On jury selection, see summary in Herbert Jacob, *Justice in America*, 2nd ed. (Boston: Little, Brown and Co., 1972), pp. 121–33; for an analysis of behavior of juries in criminal cases see Harry Kalven Jr. and Hans Zeisel, *The American Jury* (Boston: Little, Brown and Co., 1966).

a significant impact on the large number of cases disposed of by plea bargaining.

INTER-CITY VARIATION IN THE CRIMINAL PROCESS

The prevalence of the dispositional process is widely recognized. Most knowledgable observers estimate that 90 per cent of all criminal cases are settled by a guilty plea in the United States. However, behind this approximate average lurk many variations. Examine, for instance, the data for California and Wisconsin presented in Table 6.1. In California, Los Angeles utilizes the dispositional process much less than the rest of the state. In the rest of the state, 85 per cent of all criminal cases filed in Superior Court are disposed by guilty pleas; in Los Angeles only 55 per cent of the defendants plead guilty. This percentage is the consequence of a local usage which apparently prevails only in Los Angeles.[34] It is local custom to present much of the evidence at the preliminary hearing and then to try the defendants on the basis of the preliminary hearing transcript before a judge at a later time. Such trials are not full-blown adversary hearings but neither are they pure dispositional proceedings. In San Francisco, by contrast, 94 per cent of all defendants plead guilty, a proportion much closer to the norm for the state.

In Wisconsin, more detailed information is available and reveals more complex patterns. The five largest cities have almost identical patterns for the disposition of misdemeanors. Most misdemeanors are disposed by guilty pleas; only Milwaukee uses guilty pleas substantially less frequently than the other cities. The proportion of guilty pleas in the large cities is approximately the same as in the most rural counties with the extraordinary exception of Bayfield County. Note, however, the strikingly small number of misdemeanor dispositions in Kenosha and Brown Counties and the disproportionately large number in Racine. These findings may well reflect the substantially different police policies in the setting of distinctive political cultures in Kenosha and Green Bay. These cities have much more traditional political cultures than Racine and Madison; many decisions are removed from the governmental arena in the traditional cultures of Kenosha and Green Bay that elsewhere are the object of political conflict.[35] As we shall see in the next chapter, those cities also handle some civil cases quite differently than do Racine and Madison.

Felony dispositions display a different pattern. Milwaukee and Madison handle felonies quite differently than the other cities. Only one-fifth of

[34] Graham and Letwin, "The Preliminary Hearing in Los Angeles."
[35] Robert R. Alford (with the collaboration of Harry M. Scoble), *Bureaucracy and Participation* (Chicago: Rand McNally & Co., 1969), pp. 144–51.

TABLE 6.1 CASE DISPOSITIONS IN SELECTED CALIFORNIA AND
WISCONSIN CITIES AND COUNTIES

Dispositions in California Superior Courts, 1968–69*

County	Population	Total Dispositions	Dispositions before Trial Number	Percentage
Amador	11,821	12	8	67
Glenn	17,521	37	36	97
Yuba	44,736	73	66	90
Santa Barbara	264,324	585	439	75
Kern	329,162	589	498	85
San Francisco	715,674	2,716	2,550	94
Alameda	1,073,184	2,681	2,119	79
San Diego	1,357,184	3,357	3,007	89
Los Angeles	7,032,075	30,556	16,709	55
State total		58,510	40,355	69
State total minus Los Angeles		27,954	23,646	85

Felony Dispositions by Wisconsin Courts, 1969**

Adams	9,234	7	7	100
Burnett	9,276	84	84	100
Bayfield	11,683	7	0	0
Kenosha	117,917	186	160	86
Brown (Green Bay)	158,244	226	195	86
Racine	170,838	388	323	83
Dane (Madison)	290,272	406	111	27
Milwaukee	1,054,063	2,550	543	21
State total		7,385	4,286	84

Misdemeanor Dispositions by Wisconsin Courts, 1969**

Adams	9,234	201	197	98
Burnett	9,276	145	145	100
Bayfield	11,683	171	6	4
Kenosha	117,917	487	476	98
Brown (Green Bay)	158,244	461	427	93
Racine	170,838	4,295	3,871	90
Dane (Madison)	290,272	2,985	2,525	85
Milwaukee	1,054,272	8,522	6,118	72
State total		39,324	33,056	84

* Judicial Council of California, Annual Report of the Administrative Office of the California Courts, January 5, 1970, p. 146.
** State of Wisconsin Judicial Council, 1969 Judicial Statistics, pp. B54–B59.
Population figures are from 1970 census.

all felonies in Milwaukee and one-fourth of them in Madison are processed with guilty pleas; the remainder go to trial. The other cities and the rural areas are as loath to utilize trials for felonies as they are for misdemeanors. The variations evident in the detailed statistics for California and Wisconsin are also apparent in data for other large cities throughout the United States. Table 6.2 shows the most authoritative available estimates of the disposition of felonies for six major metropolitan centers in the United States; the data are averaged over the years from 1965 to 1969. If we examine only the employment of guilty pleas and trials, we find that guilty pleas predominate in Brooklyn, Detroit, and Houston whereas trials are most common in Los Angeles (as already indicated in Table 6.1) and Baltimore. In Baltimore, four-fifths of all felony indictments are tried; by contrast, trials are used in only one-twentieth of all felony indictments in Houston.[36]

It is probably misleading, however, to focus entirely on how courts make *final* dispositions, even though these outcomes provide the statistics most frequently cited in public discussion. Table 6.2 exhibits other important variations. The proportion of felony charges dropped or reduced varies as much as the use of the guilty plea. In Baltimore (where most cases are tried), most felony charges are affirmed by indictment; there is little plea bargaining prior to final disposition. Contrast this practice with Chicago and Brooklyn where three-fourths of all felony charges are either reduced to misdemeanors or dropped altogether. In Los Angeles, Detroit, and Houston, too, more cases are reduced or dropped than pursued to final disposition.

The third significant variation shown in Table 6.2 concerns the number of felony arrests made in each city. Detroit police make three times as many felony arrests as their Chicago counterparts. If we took the arrest rates as indicators of the incidence of crime (which we cannot, of course), Chicago would appear to be the safest, least crime-ridden city of the six— a strange characterization of a city famous for its mob wars and crime-infested neighborhoods. To some degree, there may be a real difference in the incidence of serious crime; Detroit includes less of the urban fringe where crime is lower than Cook County. But varying police practices probably account for most of the difference. In Chicago, it takes more serious action to be charged with a felony than in the other cities; a greater proportion of those arrested are arrested for misdemeanors. The same seems to occur in Brooklyn. In Detroit, Los Angeles, Houston, and Baltimore, police and prosecutors are quicker to charge a felony.

   [36] For similar data for New Orleans in the 1950's, see Herbert Jacob, "Politics and Criminal Prosecution in New Orleans," in *Studies in Judicial Politics*, ed. Kenneth N. Vines and Herbert Jacob (New Orleans: Tulane University Studies in Political Science, 1962), pp. 77–98.

TABLE 6.2 AVERAGE APPROXIMATE DISPOSITIONS IN SELECTED
METROPOLITAN AREAS, 1965–69

	Cook County (Chicago)	Los Angeles	Kings County (Brooklyn, NY)	Detroit	Baltimore	Harris County (Houston)
Felony arrests/ 10,000 pop.	40	96	63	118	82	89
Per cent of arrests leading to indict- ments or informa- tion	23	31	20	45	81	44
Per cent of indict- ments or informa- tion dropped or reduced to mis- demeanors	77	69	80	55	19	56
Per cent guilty pleas of all in- dicted	45	44	83	53	14	79
Per cent trials of all indicted	18	49	12	10	79	5

SOURCE: McIntyre and Lippman, *Prosecutors and Early Disposition of Felony Cases,*
pp. 1156–57.

    The data in Table 6.2, therefore, suggest several quite different kinds
of city policies with respect to serious crime. One type is the city with
strict police and with adversary judicial proceedings. This kind of city is
exemplified by Baltimore. The second type is the city with strict police
but with dispositional proceedings. Some of these cities dispose of most
cases through charge reduction or dismissal (e.g., Los Angeles) whereas
others dispose of their cases through greater use of guilty pleas. Finally,
the third type of city possesses a relatively lenient police department
which makes relatively few felony arrests; such police practices are coupled
with heavy reliance on the dispositional process. The third type of city
is exemplified by Chicago and Brooklyn. These patterns are summarized
in Figure 6.1.
    The police arrest variations shown in Table 6.2 and Figure 6.1 may
be related to the degree to which police forces follow legalistic or watch-
men styles, although both Chicago and New York (from which Brooklyn

FIGURE 6.1   Cities Classified According to Court Proceedings and
Arrest Policies

Court Proceedings	Arrest Policies	
	High Proportion of Felony Arrests	Low Proportion of Felony Arrests
Adversary	Baltimore	
Dispositional	Los Angeles Detroit Houston	Chicago Brooklyn*

* Brooklyn, of course, is not an independent city but is one of the five boroughs of New York. However, it has its own court system which has been researched more thoroughly than the court systems of other sections of New York City.

receives its police services) have highly professionalized and recently reformed police departments and, therefore, probably characterize Wilson's service style more than the watchman style. The degree to which cities depend on dispositional rather than adversary proceedings seems to be a matter of otherwise unexplained historical accident. No one has advanced a theory that explains Baltimore's heavy use of trials or the Los Angeles practice of trying defendants on the basis of preliminary hearing transcripts.[37] Although a New Orleans study showed that different prosecutors produced somewhat different conviction rates and that Negroes were increasingly discriminated against between 1954 and 1960,[38] we have too little data to conclude that strong associations exist between social or governmental characteristics of cities and their dependence on adversary or dispositional processes. However, the data from both California and Wisconsin at least suggest that size of community is not usually the principal factor in that choice. Smaller communities with fewer criminal cases use dispositional proceedings as frequently as larger cities. Indeed, if substantial reliance on adversary proceedings is now a deviant characteristic, this deviance seems to be isolated in large cities rather than small ones.

Other inter-city variations become evident when examining the man-

[37] Pittsburgh and Philadelphia are other cities relying heavily on adversary proceedings according to Alschuler, "The Prosecutor's Role." For practices in Washington, see Harry I. Subin, *Criminal Justice in a Metropolitan Court*, (Washington: Office of Criminal Justice, United States Department of Justice, 1966).
[38] Jacob, "Politics and Criminal Prosecution."

ner in which various cities handled riots that occurred in the 1960's. The major riots—in Watts (Los Angeles) in 1965; in Detroit, Newark, and many other cities during the summer of 1967; in Washington and Chicago among others after the assassination of Dr. Martin Luther King, Jr., in April 1968—imposed severe strains on the police and on the criminal courts. The Detroit riot in 1967, for instance, generated 7,231 arrests in a single week, half of the entire case load of the court in the previous year.[39] Although the burden was uniformly great, city responses varied considerably.

Most large city court systems responded to the immediate riot situation by imposing de facto preventive detention on almost all arrestees. During the 1967 riot in Detroit, for instance, most judges arbitrarily imposed bonds of $10,000 for curfew violations and higher bonds for more serious charges. The proceeding at which this imposition took place epitomized assembly-line justice. One set of observers recorded it in the following way:

> Lining up a group of fifteen or twenty unrepresented persons before the bench, the judge said, "You're accused of entering without breaking, your bond is $10,000, your examination is set for August 1." Calling the next group, he continued, "You heard what I said to them, the same applies to you." [40]

The presiding judge of the court in which these proceedings took place, later defended these practices in the following terms: [40]

> When should those arrested be released—at the time of arraignment, that night, or the next day? How can the judge know anything about any of the vast numbers arrested during a riot, whether any have a prior police record, whether any are fugitives, or whether any are already on parole for prior offenses? Is it unreasonable to delay the release of arrestees pending the setting of reasonable bonds? When should bonds be set? Should reasonable bonds even be considered during a riot conflagration? Is there a morale problem for those entrusted with the safety of the community— the police, the National Guard, and the Army—if after the arrest and delivery of an individual to the courts, the policeman or guardsman returns to the streets only to be confronted with the same person whom he recently arrested? All you need is one or two such incidents before the story spreads throughout the police or National Guard forces. Under the

---

[39] "Administration of Justice in the Wake of the Detroit Civil Disorder of July, 1967," University of Michigan Law Review, LXVI (1968), 1557.

[40] Quoted in "Administration of Justice in the Wake of the Detroit Civil Disorder," pp. 1547–48. Reprinted by permission of the publisher.

circumstances, many policemen would probably drop their badges and go home, saying, "To hell with it."[41]

Other large city court systems, however, responded somewhat differently to such circumstances. In Chicago, many defendants found themselves facing the same kind of summary proceeding as typified Detroit: For instance, consider the following transcript of a bond proceeding:

THE CLERK:	(Announcing the case)
THE STATE'S ATTORNEY:	State curfew, your honor.
THE COURT:	What were you doing on the corner?
DEFENDANT:	Going home.
THE COURT:	From where?
DEFENDANT:	From a friend's house.
THE COURT:	Thousand dollar bond. . . .[42]

Yet 71 per cent of the defendants were released without monetary bond on their own recognizance when charged such curfew offenses, and 25 per cent of all arrestees were released on their own recognizance. For half of all arrestees, the median bail required less than $100 actual cash.[43] However, even those released on recognizance or low bond were usually held in jail overnight. Thus, even in Chicago, 42 per cent of all arrestees were held in custody for more than two days.[44] In Washington, D.C., the record was about the same as in Chicago.

In smaller riot-torn cities, bonds were often set much lower, and many persons were released immediately after their original court appearance. In Newark, bail was set at $500 for curfew violations and $250 for loitering—much higher than usual but not as high as in Detroit. In Dayton, Ohio, and New Haven, Connecticut, most arrestees were released on their own recognizance throughout the riot period.[45]

City police and courts responded in varying ways to the riots. Chicago police and prosecutors engaged in considerable planning after the Los Angeles riots of 1965 and Detroit riots of 1967; one element of their plan

---

41 Vincent J. Brennan, "Proper Handling of Mass Arrests: The Experience of Two Cities: Detroit. A Response," *Denver Law Journal*, XLVI (1969), 54. Copyright by Denver Law Journal, 1969. Reprinted by permission of the publisher and author.

42 "Criminal Justice in Extremis: Administration of Justice During the April 1968 Chicago Disorder," *University of Chicago Law Review*, XXXVI (1969), 515. Reprinted by permission of the publisher.

43 "Criminal Justice in Extremis," p. 507.

44 "Criminal Justice in Extremis," p. 505.

45 *Report of the National Advisory Commission on Civil Disorders* [The Kerner Commission], (New York: Bantam Books, 1968), pp. 341–42.

was to arrest fewer rioters and charge fewer of them with felonies. Thus, as in normal times, the Chicago police performed their gatekeeping role and did not overburden the courts to the same degree as was true for the earlier riots in Los Angeles and Detroit.[46]

The subsequent processing of rioters through the court systems reflected such differences in police practice. Most of those arrested and charged in Chicago were subsequently tried and found guilty.

In Los Angeles and Detroit, by contrast, a very large proportion of cases were dismissed at the preliminary hearing stage or just before trial. Quite contrary to the normal procedure where the further the defendant is processed the more likely his eventual conviction becomes, riot cases in Los Angeles and Detroit were more likely to be dismissed the further they were processed. Eventual dismissal for a very large proportion of the cases was the only way that these court systems were able to adapt themselves to the work-load imposed by major riots.[47] The same occurred in Washington, D.C., where most persons arrested were released by the police before any court appearance; only 1,675 of the 7,600 persons arrested were brought to court.[48]

One interesting explanation of the differences among cities in the ways that their police and court systems responded to minor (but not major) riots is proposed by Isaac Balbus.[49] He notes that power is most concentrated in Chicago in the hands of the Daley machine whereas it is most dispersed in Los Angeles; Detroit lies in between. Hence in Chicago, the police and court systems could be most readily directed to a pre-selected course of action. Defendants were less likely to win release before trial, were more likely to be charged with serious crimes and more often received harsh penalties than normal defendants in Chicago or than defendants from minor riots in Los Angeles and Detroit.

DISTRIBUTIONS OF SANCTIONS

It would be foolish to suggest that the burden of sanctions should fall equally on all elements of a city's population. The purpose of the criminal process is to isolate persons who violate the law in ways perceived as

[46] Isaac D. Balbus, "Rebellion and Response: A Comparative Study of the Administration of Justice following Urban Ghetto Revolts in Three American Cities," Ph. D. dissertation, University of Chicago, 1970, pp. 498–564.
[47] Balbus, "Rebellion and Response," pp. 498–564.
[48] P. W. Chemnick, "Response of the Washington, D. C. Community and Its Criminal Justice System to the April 1968 Riot," *George Washington Law Review*, XXXVII (1969), pp. 862–1012. Note that the peace demonstrations that occurred in May, 1971, were handled in the same way.
[49] Balbus, "Rebellion and Response," pp. 534–42.

serious by the governing coalition of the community. As we showed earlier, the incidence of crime is skewed, with lower-status groups in the population more heavily involved in officially recognized crime than higher-status groups. However, the two processes by which courts deal with offenders may result in burdening various elements of the criminal population differentially. Although the evidence is not complete, it seems that this conjecture may be true.

One consequence of a city's reliance on the dispositional process is that it transfers sanctioning authority from judges to prosecutors and to the police. Where the dispositional process predominates, the police make the major decisions about sanctions by deciding whether to pull someone into the machinery of justice. Once a person is enmeshed, he rarely escapes unscathed. Even if his case is dismissed, the defendant usually has suffered one night in jail and has acquired a police record that may follow him until he dies, obstructing his efforts to obtain better employment and making each subsequent brush with the law more dangerous. Even such a brief involvement with the criminal prosecution process is likely to be a punishing experience, because none of the officials who staff the jails or courtrooms are noted for their empathy. They are concerned mostly with doing their job and not with helping someone entrapped in their proceedings. The safest strategy for an innocent person is to go along and to pretend guilt, because protestations of innocence will cause officials to label him as a troublemaker and lead to harsher treatment. Where the dispositional process is the predominant one, everyone is treated as guilty to some degree; everyone whom the police insert into the system is punished.

Consequently, the biases which influence police action continue to affect all subsequent proceedings. Since no city in the United States employs a pure adversary process, all persons arrested suffer from some of the effects of being treated as if they were guilty. However, where adversary proceedings are more prominent, the safeguards of the adversary system may provide more effective protection for the innocent enmeshed in the process.

Most cities employ elements of both systems, and it is this coexistence that probably produces the most biased results. Where defendants have a choice of proceedings, those with substantial resources can most effectively choose either to bargain for a dismissal or to go to court and win an acquittal at trial. But such a strategy is possible only for persons who can afford a private attorney and who can endow him with an investigative apparatus. The ordinary defendant is too poor to do that; he relies on the public defender or assigned counsel who must presume the guilt of his client and bargain for a minimal sentence in order to maintain efficiency in his defense operations. If the poor defendant insists on a trial, he takes an inordinate risk of conviction and extra harsh sentence. Because resources are so important in providing initial release from jail while awaiting trial and later in effective bargaining with the prosecutor, those with the fewest resources are the most likely to become poor parole risks while they are in jail awaiting trial. Thus, the poor are the most frequent recipients of prison sentences while persons who are not poor more frequently receive suspended sentences or parole.[50]

There are additional consequences to the availability of choice of two rather than one type of criminal proceeding. The dispositional process maximizes the influence of officials who may be closely linked to partisan politics in the city, because it increases the influence of the police (who are under the control of an elected mayor) and of the prosecutor (who is elected on a partisan ballot).[51] The influence of judges (who are somewhat more remote from partisan politics) is minimized. Consequently, the dispositional process may be more responsive to the winds of political change. Cities relying mostly on the dispositional process may more readily shift their attention from one crime to another or from one group of offenders to another because change of focus mostly involves shifting the activities of the police and changing the policies of the prosecutor. In cities where the adversary process more fully predominates, police actions have less significance because offenders would not be treated as guilty until the courts (judges) had found them guilty. Therefore, police would be relegated to the role of initiators of a process whose outcome was problematic rather than as initial avengers whose preliminary punishment is certain to be confirmed in later proceedings.

In most cities, however, the link between community sentiment and punishment of "criminals" by police and courts is a tenuous one. Most of the public is unaware of the true characteristics of the criminal prosecution process; few channels exist to link public opinion with court action. Consequently, a few strategically located influentials who interest themselves in courtroom actions can exert influence on the mayor, chief of police, or prosecutor.[52] But the process remains isolated from the general public—not because it is apolitical, but because it is too well disguised for effective public action.

---

[50] Banfield and Anderson, "Continuances"; Wettick, "Assignment of Judges."
[51] For possible influence of election process on prosecutors, see Jacob, "Politics and Criminal Prosecution," pp. 89–90, 95–96.
[52] Compare Balbus, "Rebellion and Response"; Levin, "Urban Political Systems and Judicial Behavior"; John A. Gardiner, The Politics of Corruption: Organized Crime in an American City (New York: Russell Sage Foundation, 1970).

seven

THE DISPOSITION
OF
CIVIL CASES

Civil cases usually attract less attention from the media and the general public. These cases often appear to involve only private individuals, or they revolve around complex and seemingly abstract points of law. But as we saw earlier, they too may determine important distributions of wealth, welfare, and power in the city.

The disposition of civil cases is set in the same framework of legal procedures as the criminal prosecution process. The rules and rituals vary somewhat, but many of the same legal assumptions apply. As with the criminal prosecution process, the adversarial and the dispositional model provide alternative perspectives. Neither dominates completely; each is modified (to varying degrees in different kinds of cases) by the presence of the other.

The adversarial model is the model which most affects the formal procedures governing the disposition of civil cases. A civil suit begins with the filing of a complaint with the clerk of a court. The complaint lists the plaintiff's grievances against the defendant; it also asks the courts to remedy the situation by ordering the defendant to compensate the plaintiff or to make other reparation as provided by law. In order for a court to entertain such a complaint, the plaintiff must show that he has been or is about to be harmed by the defendant and that the law (either by statute or by common-law) provides a remedy that the courts may invoke. The complaint is served on the defendant, and he usually has a month to reply. His reply may consist of a simple denial of the allegations, a defense of his action, or the contention that the courts lack jurisdiction; in addition it may include counter-allegations that it is really the defendant who has been harmed and not the plaintiff. If the defendant makes a counter complaint, the plaintiff is given time to respond to it. When all the complaints, replies, and cross-complaints have been filed and answered, the issue is said to be joined and ready for disposition in court. But the case is not ready for trial. Each side's attorneys must prepare their cases by collecting relevant facts from documents and witnesses. Most of this work involves taking depositions from witnesses and inspecting documents in the possession of either the plaintiff or defendant. In many states and in federal courts, extensive discovery procedures are available through which the plaintiff may obtain documents and may interview witnesses who appear to support the defense claims, and the defendant may obtain similar information from the plaintiff. As a result of such forays into the evidence supporting the opposing case, lawyers can usually assess the evidentiary strength of the opposing case. Many facts are undisputed and can be agreed upon before the trial.

In many jurisdictions, pre-trial conferences have become an important part of the formal procedure.[1] When the case is called for trial, the judge directs opposing counsel to confer with each other (sometimes in the presence of the judge) in order to reach an agreement about undisputed facts, to narrow the issues of fact and law which the trial shall consider, and to seek a negotiated settlement. If the pre-trial conference does not produce a settlement or if no pre-trial conference occurred, the case goes to trial before a judge or before a judge and a jury. Although juries are commonly available, most civil cases are heard by judges alone because litigants prefer to avoid the cost of jury trials, because of the often greater uncertainty about jury decisions, and because of the delays which often attend jury trials. Even with a jury trial, judges have a greater voice in civil cases than in criminal dispositions. They may limit the jury's decision to fact finding and reserve to themselves the details of the compensation or other remedies which may be justified by the jury's decision.

Throughout these formal proceedings, the assumptions of the adversary proceeding prevail. The object of the proceedings is to discover the truth. To win his case, the plaintiff must show that the preponderance of the evidence support his claims. As in criminal cases, the proceeding is staged as a two-sided conflict. Other sides may enter (if at all) only on

---

[1] The most complete study of pre-trial conferences is Maurice Rosenberg, The Pre-trial Conference and Effective Justice (New York: Columbia University Press, 1964).

behalf of the plaintiff or defendant. Evidentiary rules and rules of procedure have been developed to optimize the search for truth with heavy reliance on eye-witness, first-hand accounts of events. The search for truth is conceived as a simple task that any reasonable man may master successfully. As a result, jurors are not required to have any special qualifications; indeed, they are usually disqualified if they possess expertise in the field of the suit because the adversarial assumption that such expertise creates prejudgments rather than an open mind which may understand the dispute better. Likewise, most judges possess no particular expertise in the cases they hear. On one day a judge may decide a brace of marital disputes; the next day, he may be preoccupied with a complex real estate transaction.

However, as with the criminal prosecution process, most cases are not decided by procedures which follow the prescriptions of the adversary process. Most cases are settled out of court. In many instances, indeed, filing a complaint in court is only a notice to the other side that the plaintiff is serious about his claim. Legal action leads to negotiation and settlement. In other instances, some of the rituals of the adversary proceeding are followed, but they are a guise to a pre-formulated settlement that the court will legitimate in due course.

Negotiations for out-of-court settlements are routine in most cases; they often exclude judges and other court personnel. If both parties agree to a settlement, they simply let their court suit die from non-prosecution. The reasons for the prevalence of out-of-court settlements are numerous. The expense and delay involved in going to trial encourage many litigants to negotiate. In addition, both parties retain control over the shape of the settlement and protect the privacy of their files in negotiated settlements; in court they must make their evidence public and invite outsiders such as judges or jurors to determine their fate. However, the availability of a full-fledged adversary proceeding imposes constraints on settlements, because few disputants will agree to a settlement considerably less advantageous than an expected court decision.

Out-of-court settlements have been most fully studied in personal-injury suits.[2] Insurance companies are the normal defendants in such suits; they routinely seek to obtain an out-of-court settlement for all but the largest claims because they find settlements cheaper to administer and often smaller than court awards. A very important variable, however, is whether the plaintiff (the injured party) has the services of an attorney. When the claimant has no attorney, compensation payments are usually

[2] See especially H. Laurence Ross, *Settled out of Court* (Chicago: Aldine Publishing Co., 1970), pp. 73–86, 136–75.

smaller than when claimants are represented professionally. A lawyer, of course, costs a considerable amount of money—usually one-quarter to one-third of the compensation award. But even when the fee is paid, represented claimants usually obtain more money from the insurance company than unrepresented ones.[3] This advantage may change when no-fault insurance becomes more common in the United States, but in jurisdictions where the injured party makes his claim against the other driver's insurance company, representation by an attorney in out-of-court settlements is important in optimizing compensation payments. The ease with which one can negotiate with a company and the size of the payment also vary with the insurance company.[4] Insurance companies always utilize the services of lawyers. Many claims agents are attorneys, and they always have access to a legal department for advice. Claims agents are instructed in the intricacies of tort liability law so that they can effectively negotiate with claimants directly or with claimants' attorneys.[5]

Although most personal-injury claims are negotiated out of court, personal-injury suits remain one of the major categories of claims brought to court. In addition, personal-injury suits represent a major portion of court backlog and a substantial portion of all cases which go to trial.[6] Trials—and the adversarial process—are frequently used because liability laws provide a good defense for offending motorists and their insurance companies. In most states, when a complainant has contributed to the accident through a bit of his own carelessness, strict interpretation of the law denies him compensation. Since there are many instances of possible contributory negligence, a substantial number of cases go to trial. But even when there may be a contributory negligence, most insurance companies find it cheaper to pay off small claims than to go to trial; usually, only the largest claims find their way to the courts. Large claims sometimes go to trial even when liability is clear because no one in the insurance company is willing to authorize a large payment by himself. The court judgment shields insurance executives from charges of being careless with company funds.[7]

A different mix of the dispositional and adversarial processes exists in divorce cases. All divorces (except in states where no-fault divorce is available, as in California) must be brought to court in an adversary proceeding. One spouse is the plaintiff who charges the other with fault in the marital breakup and seeks a divorce. The defendant may file a cross-

[3] Ibid., pp. 193–98.

[4] "Auto Insurance: The Quality Factor," *Consumer Reports*, XXXV (1970), 332–41.

[5] Ross, *Settled out of Court*, pp. 27–41.

[6] Hans Zeisel, Harry Kalven Jr., and Bernard Buchholz, *Delay in the Courts*, (Boston: Little, Brown and Co., 1963).

[7] Ross, *Settled out of Court*, pp. 220–22.

complaint. If both parties are found at fault, a judge may deny both of them a divorce.

The adversarial pose of divorce proceedings, however, is only a guise for extensive out-of-court negotiations which pre-determine the outcome of the court hearing; the trial only legitimates the negotiated settlement.[8] In many divorce proceedings, there is substantial (if reluctant) agreement by both parties that the marriage should be terminated. The most contested claims concern alimony, division of property, custody of children, visitation rights, and child-support payments. These issues each involve complex legal, emotional, and social problems; but they are usually negotiable. Both spouses have attorneys; their attorneys handle the negotiations and draft the divorce decree. When the case comes to court, most divorces are uncontested, and the testimony brought to court is carefully prepared so that it provides sufficient support for a favorable judgment by the court. The draft decree is then presented to the judge, and in most cases he signs it without change. The negotiated settlement thus is legitimized by court action; adversarial rituals disguise a dispositional proceeding.

Other civil suits involve similar guises for prior private agreements. Many consumer installment sales include agreements signed by the customer that he will not contest a judgment suit brought by the seller or the lender if the customer falls behind in his payments.[9] Consequently, when retailers go to court to obtain judgments against customers who have stopped their installment payments, the businessmen simply file their papers and win default judgments. They may then return to court to win the right to seize some of the customer's property or his wages in order to obtain payment of the debt, or they may sometimes repossess the purchased item without court action. In most instances, the defendants of these suits make no effort to defend themselves and have had (until recent consumer legislation changed the law somewhat) little legal ground to assert a defense. The outcome of the suit was in fact settled when the defendant made the purchase and signed the agreements.[10]

The dispositional processes which govern the outcome of most civil cases may perhaps be best conceptualized as group decision-making processes. This viewpoint is in contrast to the normal perception of the adversarial process in which the decision-maker is the single judge who

---

[8] Hubert O'Gorman, Lawyers and Matrimonial Cases (New York: The Free Press, 1963); Doris J. Freed and Henry H. Foster, Jr., "Divorce American Style." Annals of the American Academy of Political and Social Science, CCCLXXXIII (1969), 71–88.

[9] This type of agreement is called "confession of judgment."

[10] The fullest discussion of these practices are by David Caplovitz, Debtors in Default (New York: Columbia University Bureau of Applied Social Research, 1972, mimeo), Chapters 11–13; Herbert Jacob, Debtors in Court (Chicago: Rand McNally & Co., 1969), pp. 73–86.

presides over the trial court.[11] When one views decision-making in civil cases as a dispositional process, the single judge of the trial is joined by a large group of other participants who generally have a greater voice in the decision than the judge. The most important participants are the attorneys for the plaintiff and defendant; they are joined in particular cases by clerical personnel of the court and by auxiliaries of each litigant. In a few cases, a jury is added to the decision-making group. Unlike most small decision-making groups, the ones that determine the outcome of civil cases have no permanence. But interactions between particular sets of attorneys before specific judges occur with considerable frequency. A relatively small set of lawyers is involved in most personal injury settlements; a different set of attorneys handles most divorce cases; still different sets of attorneys handle the probate of wills or collection suits. Attorneys in each set develop working relations with each other and norms that specify expected behaviors which will promote settlements. Attorneys with little experience in one of these fields encounter difficulty in negotiating a settlement because they have not been socialized into the norms of the decision-making group.

There are important differences between the groups that dominate decision-making in civil cases and those that control the process in criminal cases. The groups in civil cases are more ad hoc and involve a larger number of private attorneys than in the criminal sphere. Most criminal cases are handled by a small subset that is in continual contact; contact is more occasional among those handling civil cases. Fewer of the decision-makers are public officials in civil cases. Whereas the prosecutor is almost always involved in the disposition of criminal cases, and the judge is often involved, at least in a ritualistic manner, many settlements of civil cases involve no public official. Another difference is that civil cases often involve large organizations. The organizational characteristics of the litigants may play a large role in the negotiation process by determining the amount of flexibility permitted and the tolerance of the client for courtroom hearings rather than settlements.[12] By contrast, most criminal cases involve single individuals as defendants with a small bureaucracy—the prosecutor's office—as plaintiff.

[11] For instance, Ulmer only considers appellate courts as involving small groups: S. Sidney Ulmer, "The Courts as Small and Not-So-Small Groups," (New York: General Learning Corporation, 1971).

[12] Jacob, Debtors in Court, pp. 78–84; Stewart Macauley, Law and the Balance of Power (New York: Russell Sage Foundation, 1965).

CIVIL CASES AND URBAN POLITICS

The range of civil cases is immense. They may involve almost any element of personal life; they may also concern almost any public issue, public official, or governmental agency in the urban environment. The political involvement of courts in civil cases depends on both the characteristics of the litigants and the issues they raise in their litigation. The litigants may range from private individuals to government officials; the issues may range from disputes that are perceived by most people as entailing only private relationships to conflicts that most observers agree involve public policy.

FIGURE 7.1   Typology of Civil Cases.

Plaintiffs	ISSUES	
	Private	Public
	I	III
Private	Divorce, personal injury, collection, etc.	Suits challenging zoning, desegregation, welfare program decisions
	II	IV
Public	Divorce, personal injury, collection involving public figures Evictions from public housing projects	Suits over apportionment of funds, elections, antipollution, antitrust

The first category of civil cases involves private individuals in disputes that most people perceive as embracing only private matters. The best-known examples are personal-injury suits and divorce cases; others are collection suits, disputes between businessmen over contracts, contests over wills, and disputes over land. All these matters may entail significant matters of public policy, because the legal rules invoked by litigants help some groups to obtain their objectives and hinder others. Collectively, such litigation redistributes billions of dollars each year. Nevertheless, most such cases are perceived as "private" by litigants, the courts, and the public.

Such cases embrace a very large segment of the public. The most numerous of these cases—personal-injury suits, divorce cases, and disputes over consumer purchases—arise out of incidents that may occur to almost anyone. Everyone in the city hazards involvement in such cases with almost equal risk; for automobile accidents occur almost by chance in crowded city streets and expressways; marital disputes occur with almost equal frequency among most social groups; and almost everyone (even the poor) may become entangled in a dispute with a merchant or lender over the purchase of some product. Thus, there are few class biases in the incidence of the situations that cause these disputes. However, they do not reach court in equal proportions across all categories of citizens. People who have the most at stake and can best afford attorneys, court costs, and the other burdens of litigation are most likely to bring their private disputes into court. Consequently, the largest personal-injury cases and divorce cases involving considerable property settlements are more likely to go to formal trial rather than be settled out of court. On the other hand, collection suits are most likely to be directed against working-class or poor defendants who are unable to defend themselves adequately in court battles; in such cases merchants use the courts to their own advantage in an unequal struggle.

Another characteristic of these disputes is that few of the participants seek to expand the conflict into the public arena. Although their conflict embraces matters of public [13] law, they rarely challenge the law but rather seek an application of it. They seldom expand their case to a class action; their case almost never attracts interest-group attention or *amicus curiae* briefs. When they do (e.g., some of the litigation is sponsored by neighborhood legal clinics), traditionalists protest the "politicization" of the legal process.

Because most of the participants in these disputes perceive them as private, the cases rarely spill over into the political arena. Public officials (aside from judicial staff) remain aloof from them; they do not become part of the agenda of public bodies. Even the media ignore them, so that only persons directly involved in the disputes know of their existence and of the court decisions. However, because their incidence is related to social circumstances which give rise to them, they are related to the social and economic characteristics of cities. Large cities are notorious for having more automobile accidents (witness the higher premium rates) than small ones; cities with very large populations of old people have

---

[13] These are matters of "public" law in the sense that the law is the product of legislation and litigation rather than the private rules of a single group. However, most people perceive these conflicts as private, and most lawyers call the body of such laws "private" law.

lower divorce rates. In addition, some research has suggested that the public culture of the city also affects the incidence of wage-garnishment suits and personal-bankruptcy actions.[14] In cities with more traditional modes of doing public and private business, such litigation is less frequent than in cities with more modern, bureaucratic styles of transacting public and private business. Political characteristics, such as the absence of city managers in traditional cities and their presence in modern, bureaucratic ones, do not affect such litigation but are the result of the same forces which in one case depress its incidence and in the other case, promote it.

The second category of civil cases involves public figures in disputes over private matters. These are the cases that supply the grist of the gossip's mill: divorce actions, bankruptcies, wills, personal-injury suits involving public celebrities. These actions are almost the only "private" civil cases that the media report. Their public significance lies entirely in the characteristics of one or both of the litigants—the fact that they hold important positions in the city's political life. Litigants, however, try to regard such disputes as private and they make as little effort as others to enlarge the public scope of the court action. Their public significance lies in the effect that a court decision has on the career of the litigants. In a few cases unfavorable court outcomes may seriously cripple political ambitions, but that is less true now than it was a half century ago.

Another set of civil cases in this second category involves public agencies seeking judicial remedies against private citizens. For instance, public-housing authorities are constantly in court to evict undesirable tenants; units of government that levy property taxes seek court permission to sell property of delinquent taxpayers. The remedies are usually considered private and attract little attention. However, when groups with political influence find themselves the principal target of these actions (as when most public-housing tenants are black), they attempt to alter the agency's policy of seeking court orders by action in the other political arenas—for instance, by obtaining support from the mayor's office, by winning new appointments to these administrative agencies, or by raising the issue in city election campaigns.

The third category of civil cases is also initiated by private citizens but usually attacks some kind of government action or inaction such as denial or grant of zoning variance or a license, the challenge of a tax assessment, or an alleged irregularity in some government program such as for schools, welfare, or hospitals. The plaintiff often seeks private gain through a successful court action. For instance, a zoning variance may permit him to build a more profitable apartment house or shopping center,

---

[14] Jacob, *Debtors in Court*, pp. 87–96.

and a successful appeal of a tax assessment may save him millions of dollars in local property taxes.[15] Other suits of this character seek to advance a public goal—one which will benefit the people in the same situation as the litigant. Desegregation suits, for instance, typically are initiated by parents of school children; the intent is to help not only their own children but all those in the same situation. Likewise, court challenges of welfare procedures by which recipients are arbitrarily removed from the rolls may be initiated by one such client, but the goal of such a case is to change administrative procedures in all similar cases.

Such cases comprise a very small portion of the entire docket. In part of suburban Long Island, for instance, they constituted less than 1 per cent of the cases brought to the major trial court.[16] Nor do plaintiffs represent a cross-section of the population or of the governing elite. Most of the cases in the Long Island study were brought by businessmen, especially by those involved in some phase of real estate work. Among the major interests in local politics, many were absent or sparsely represented among the litigants, for instance:

BANKS: no cases initiated

NEWSPAPERS: two cases seeking to restrain labor unions

CHURCHES: several cases involving site locations for minority religions

POLICE GROUPS: no cases initiated

SHOPPING CENTERS: three tax assessment cases

UTILITIES: two cases involving site location, one involving trade name

BUSINESS ASSOCIATIONS: no cases initiated

EDUCATIONAL GROUPS: no cases initiated

REAL ESTATE BUILDERS AND DEVELOPERS: continued use of courts to free land from restrictions and permit maximum profit

MAJOR MANUFACTURERS: four cases seeking to restrain labor union activities

VETERANS: no cases initiated

CONTRACTORS: several cases by disappointed bidders.[17]

The principle which governs selection of plaintiffs in such cases is the lure of favorable government action that cannot be attained through other means. People who can obtain favorable zoning variances through normal channels or who can win beneficial rulings from an agency without going to court, never appear in the court as plaintiffs. Thus, the composi-

---

[15] Cf. Richard F. Babcock, *The Zoning Game* (Madison: University of Wisconsin Press, 1969), especially Chapters 3 and 6.

[16] Kenneth M. Dolbeare, *Trial Courts in Urban Politics* (New York: John Wiley & Sons, Inc., 1967), p. 34.

[17] Dolbeare, *Trial Courts*, p. 44.

tion of the governing coalition in a city and the characteristics of the policies they advance play an important role in suppressing (or promoting) civil litigation. Cities bent on fast growth which are dominated by real estate developers are not likely to have many zoning cases brought to court against them; cities governed by a black and white liberal coalition are unlikely to face desegregation suits. Cities with opposite characteristics are much more likely to have such cases on their court dockets.

Another distinguishing characteristic of this category of civil suits is that they are usually preceded by public conflict in another arena. Zoning cases usually are heard by zoning boards and city councils before they reach the courts; tax appeals are considered by special boards before litigation is possible. Thus, the litigation is public not only in the sense that public goods are sought but also in the sense that the prior conflict took place in public view before other governmental agencies. Court action is another step in the political struggle to obtain (or to maintain) advantageous treatment.

The public nature of such suits is also marked by the character of the participants. A substantial number of them utilize the services of "politically connected" law firms.[18] Such firms exist in many cities; they are staffed by relatives of public officials, by former officials, or by close political allies of incumbent officials. They are employed in the hope that they understand the predilections of judges (who are often former political allies) better than the ordinary lawyer; they often specialize in such cases. Moreover, such cases more often attract assistance from interest groups in the form of a financial subsidy, legal assistance, or the filing of *amicus curiae* briefs.

Contrary to most "private" civil cases, cases involving claims against public agencies generally are *not* settled out of court and are decided by a full adversary proceeding. The reason is that such suits are filed only after a long series of prior decisions which commit the city or government agency that is defending the case. If compromise is possible, it usually occurs long before the case comes to court—for instance, in negotiations with a zoning board at which the builder agrees to alter his plans in return for the variance that he is seeking. But once a zoning board or tax appeals board has rendered a formal decision, the time for compromise is past. Consequently, most of these cases go to trial before a judge or jury.

The public consequences of most of these cases is clear. Court decisions either affirm or revise the policy decisions of other public agencies. In many instances, the court's decision extends beyond the particular case because other claimants for public favors keep an eye on such court decisions. They are encouraged to press their own claims when the courts

18 Dolbeare, *Trial Courts*, pp. 71–74.

rule favorably and are inhibited when the courts deny claims similar to theirs. Fundamental policies—such as those regulating access to public facilities by racial minorities, or the right to contest bureaucratic denials of welfare applications—are routinely affected by court decisions in this category of cases. In Chicago, for instance, such a decision greatly increased pressure to scatter low-income public housing to non-ghetto areas and to the suburbs. When the city moved too slowly for the court, it froze all "model cities" funds and threatened the loss of millions of dollars of federal grants. Earlier, in New York, such a suit legitimized a referendum abolishing a civilian review board for the police department that the city had established but that police organizations thought was illegal and unfavorable to their interests.

This category of civil actions is much more closely related to city political traits than the first two. Those who possess control of legislative and administrative agencies in the city rarely have the need to sue in court; they obtain their favors directly through the normal political arena. The degree to which the governing coalition compromises with significant opposing interests affects the incidence of such suits. As long as interests that are out of power are accommodated by compromises, are hopeful of winning office themselves, or are too weak and fragmented to sponsor court action, they will not bring their cases to court. Only outsiders who have no hope for favorable action within the normal political channels bring their claims to the courtroom. The hesitance to go to court hinges in part on the lack of success in court. The Long Island study by Dolbeare found that courts decided slightly more than half of the zoning claims and two-thirds of the other cases in favor of the defending government agency.[19] Moreover, a lost court battle often forecloses later attempts to win negotiated compromises in subsequent disputes because the court decision strengthens the position of the administrative agency.

The fourth category of civil cases involves conflicts brought by public officials and involving disputes in the public realm. The defendants may be other public officials or agencies, as when a city official sues a state agency, or they may be private parties, as when civil anti-trust action is filed against a corporation.

Some of the most spectacular and significant court forays into local politics arise out of this kind of suit. For instance, disputes over the apportionment of state funds for public welfare played an important role in Chicago politics in 1971. The governor sought to balance the state budget by cutting the welfare funds allotted to Cook County and suggested that Cook County cut its welfare rolls drastically or reduce general assistance payments by two-thirds. These moves were directed against Cook County in November and were scheduled to go into effect in the rest of Illinois

---

[19] Dolbeare, Trial Courts, p. 72.

in December. The county—under the direction of Mayor Daley's political allies—brought the dispute to court and the court ruled that the governor's actions were illegal, forcing him to pay the full allotment to Cook County and other counties and to find other ways to balance the state budget. Other disputes center around the conduct of elections, the jurisdiction of local offices which are held by opposing parties or factions, and efforts to enforce anti-trust and anti-pollution laws where civil remedies are more appropriate than criminal sanctions.

Socio-economic characteristics of cities have little relation to the incidence of this kind of litigation. It is more a function of governmental structure and political division. Where governmental structure is fragmented rather than unified, jurisdictional disputes are more likely to arise and more likely to reach the courts. In many instances, of course, domination by one political coalition overcomes formal fragmentation. In Chicago, for instance, the division of power between the city, the Sanitary District, the Chicago Transit Authority, and the county provide multiple opportunities for conflict. In recent years, however, the powerful Democratic party machine organized by Mayor Daley has dominated most of these governmental bodies and has provided informal coordination and avoidance of conflict. When Republicans capture significant offices, conflict increases, and more such cases are brought to the courts. It is also well known, of course, that most judges are veterans of the Daley machine and therefore are unlikely to cause unnecessary trouble. By contrast, other cities display more open conflict between "independent" agencies and this conflict more often reaches the courts. For instance, the suburban communities in New York that Dolbeare describes were just experiencing a shift from Republican to Democratic office holders. The election for county administrator had been bitter and narrowly won. A series of spectacular court cases emerged as the conflict continued, with Republicans pursuing a holding action to retain as much patronage and decision-making power as possible while the new Democratic office holders attempted to extend their domain as quickly as they could.[20]

As with civil cases initiated by private individuals that involve public concerns, few of these cases are settled out of court. Most of the disputes are negotiated intensively behind the scenes through legislative and administrative decision-making processes before they reach the courts. When litigation is filed, it signifies the breakdown of such negotiations much as the outbreak of war follows the failure of diplomacy. When such a conflict is brought to court, positions are usually too hardened to permit compromise. In some instances, a litigant may invite court action, despite his likely defeat in court, in order to shift the onus of an unpopular decision from itself to the judiciary. This stance, for instance,

[20] Dolbeare, *Trial Courts*, pp. 45–51.

was typical of Southern school boards facing desegregation.[21] Rather than seize the initiative and formulate their own desegregation plans, they waited until they were sued and forced to desegregate under a court order.

The policy consequences of this fourth kind of civil suit are immediate, direct, and almost universally recognized. Such cases represent the clearest example of the courts' involvement in the governmental decision-making process. Depending on local circumstances, courts contribute to housing policy, school policy, transportation policy, tax policies, and almost every other disputed question in the urban environment. The courts' involvement, however, is sporadic. It is the result of the failure of other decision-making processes to accommodate significant minority views. Those out of power who find their interests seriously threatened by the decisions of the governing coalition may, as a last resort, turn to the courts for protection. The courts do not always respond favorably to such appeals but court action usually significantly delays the implementation of policies (often until another election), checks the impetus of the governing coalition's drive, and sometimes alters the policies themselves.

CONCLUSION

The link between city politics and civil litigation is not as close as that between criminal prosecutions and city politics. Every criminal case is the result of decisions by public officials; each represents the execution of an explicit public policy. By contrast, most civil cases—although settled or adjudicated under the influence of public laws—are initiated by private individuals who perceive their conflict as a private matter. Only a handful of cases involve public officials or agencies—either as defendants or as plaintiffs—embroiled in controversy over public policy in the courts. The incidence of private cases may be indirectly affected by the socio-economic characteristics of the city, since these traits are related to the incidence of conflict and the likelihood that conflict will be taken to court. But the degree of control exercised by city officials over this process is very small. By contrast, civil cases involving public policy are the direct result of governmental structure and political strife. Both the incidence of such litigation and the consequences that flow from judicial decisions are closely linked to characteristics of urban political processes. The more fragmented the policy-making process and the more divided the control exercised by the governing coalition, the more likely it is that such conflict will spill over to the courts in the form of civil litigation.

[21] Jack W. Peltason, *Fifty-eight Lonely Men* (Champaign: University of Illinois Press, 1961).

eight

CONCLUSION

Contemporary conditions pose severe challenges to the institutions which administer justice in American cities. The media multiply the impact of common crimes so that not only the actual victims but thousands of other people become conscious of the crime problem and develop a fear of strangers, darkness, and unidentified noises. At the same time, partisan politics has spilled beyond the bounds of electoral campaigns. Dissidents do not wait until the next election; they are not satisfied with a soap box in a park corner. Rather they act whenever the mood seizes them and demonstrate their feelings in ways calculated to disrupt ordinary life and draw attention to their cause. Their cause may be far removed from the urban scene, but it poses problems to urban authorities. For instance, when President Nixon mined the harbors of North Vietnam, in May, 1972, peace groups countered with "blockades" of expressways in Chicago and other urban centers. They drew four abreast and either abandoned their cars or drove at five miles per hour while thousands of commuters backed up behind them. Finally, racial, ethnic, and economic turmoil boil over in urban riots. For days, thousands of angry persons rampage through sections of the city, burning, and looting while the rest of the city quivers in fear.

Crime, political demonstrations, and riots pose severe challenges to order in the urban community. The police, prosecutors, and courts are considered by many to be the principal agencies for coping with these problems. But their function is to contain and suppress rather than to ameliorate fundamental conditions. In facing these challenges, the justice-administering agencies play a fundamentally conservative role in urban politics. Each of the challenges, however, is met in a somewhat different manner.

Routine processing procedures are the response to common crime. The amount of crime recognized by the police depends on the capacity of the courts and prisons to process defendants. The kinds of crime considered important enough to provoke police action depend on the responsiveness of the urban political system to various groups in the city. The principal driving force of the justice system, however, is the impulse to tame the workload. Considerations of due process or of other requirements of the adversarial process have become secondary. Only the rhetoric remains adversarial. For instance, in some locales, limits are imposed on the length of time that criminal cases may remain pending; after six months they must be dismissed because such a delay is said to violate due-process requirements for a speedy trial. The consequence of such a constraint, however, is not to produce more adversarial proceedings but rather to promote more plea bargaining and less concern for due process.

The dominant processing routines tend to magnify the disadvantages of economically deprived and ethnically scorned groups. Where groups lack influence with the governing coalition of the city (as is the case in most American cities), they cannot avoid becoming the special target of police action. Once the police have brought them into the justice-dispensing machinery, the processing routines provide little opportunity for unscathed escape. The result is one quite contrary to much popular opinion about the laxness of American justice. Much of the public feels that too many defendants escape with dismissals or probationary release rather than being confined in prisons for long periods of time. In fact, almost no one who is arrested by the police escapes without some stigmatization; among the poor, most suffer at least several days of imprisonment regardless of the ultimate verdict. Many lose their jobs as a consequence; and after arrest, they have a harder time finding another job. Although the justice system may be too lenient to some, it is too uniformly harsh for most defendants.

Many observers recognize these tendencies, but few reforms are directed toward remedying such inconsistencies. Every reform that attempts to reinforce the adversarial process fails because the adversarial process cannot cope with the caseload under presently conceivable resource allocations. Some reforms, on the other hand, blatantly attempt to remove the cases of the poor from the courts so that courtrooms may be used "more profitably" to decide cases involving large sums of money. To some degree this argument underlies the support of some people for no-fault insurance; it constitutes the justification for limiting access to the courts for class-action suits regarding evictions, consumer contracts, and similar causes.

The latent objective of the justice-administering agencies in coping with common crimes is to maintain the ascendancy of dominant social norms. The justice agents contribute to the maintenance of order by sustaining the legitimacy of legal norms and applying them with rituals that mask their political functions. The rituals in court serve to insulate the courts from the partisan conflicts that surround many of the norms employed in court.

That objective is much more evident in the manner that political demonstrations are dealt with. Local authorities usually discriminate blatantly between demonstrations which support the existing regime (even though the demonstrators express opposition to present office holders) and demonstrations which express opposition to the regime itself. Thus, political rallies connected with election campaigns are generally protected by the police and rarely lead to mass arrests. Marches and rallies protesting police brutality, expressing opposition to American foreign policy, or stating opposition to some local project, are much more closely policed and much more likely to lead to arrest and prosecution. The result is the criminalization of political dissidents, labelling them criminals as a result of their arrest for political activities. Their criminal acts may range from marching on the roadway rather than the sidewalk, burning draft cards, and taunting policemen to assaults on other citizens and policemen and damaging public property. On the other hand, political demonstrators often hope for arrest in order to become martyrs in the eyes of their followers and to win a forum at the time of their demonstrations and when their cases come to court. Martyrdom is important because it proves the serious intent of the demonstrators; for instance, there was a time when one was not deemed committed to the anti-war or civil rights causes unless one had spent at least one night in jail as a consequence of activities in support of these causes. But in addition, arrests produce news and, therefore, spread the message of the demonstrators far wider than any peaceful demonstration that is not picked up by the TV cameras. In court, political demonstrators are likely to insist on adversarial proceedings in order to obtain a courtroom forum. While the prosecutor attempts to limit the case to the crime of disorderly conduct or destruction of government property, the defendants seek to raise political and moral questions central to their cause.

Criminalization of political demonstrators is intended to isolate them from the political mainstream. Not only do prison terms isolate leaders for long periods of time, but they leave prison stigmatized as ordinary criminals. The political causes they espouse are tainted with criminality and made to appear illegitimate.

The order-maintenance function of justice-administering agencies is most evident when they are confronted with riots. Under riot conditions —even when martial law is not declared—police, prosecutors, many defense attorneys, and judges—join in a conspiracy to legitimize the brute force of the establishment and to suppress the riot. All those arrested are treated as if guilty; almost none are released on bail during the rioting. Although many arrests may have been unjustified, no distinction is made between the criminal offender and the innocent bystander. However, after the riot has subsided, the need to process cases reasserts itself. Justice-administering agencies then adapt themselves to the enormous caseload generated by the riots by dismissing most of the cases or by sentencing those who plead guilty to time already served in jail. But in riots, not only are the rioters stigmatized as criminals; the otherwise illegal actions of the authorities are legitimized as acceptable. False arrest and the use of undue force are not recognized as illegitimate under riot conditions.

Consequently, in most circumstances justice-administering agencies are conservative institutions whose main activity is the maintenance of the status quo. Calling them conservative does not deny their ability to adapt and change and even to force changes in other governmental institutions. But most changes coming from the courts and allied agencies are incremental accretions to existing arrangements. Few involve fundamental alterations of norms widely accepted by the existing regime. The most famous example of significant change—the court decisions regarding race relations—reasserted norms long latent in the American polity. They were hardly new or revolutionary.

It is, therefore, not surprising that the antagonism that deprived members of the society direct at other governmental institutions are also directed toward justice-administering agencies. The police are the most obvious target of these antagonisms as shown not only by the barnyard epithets hurled at them but also as revealed by one public-opinion survey after another. Courts and judges, however, do not fare significantly better. They are also perceived as instruments of the governing coalition in its effort to sustain its privileges and position. When political feelings run high and tension is great, justice-administering agencies are no more immune from those tensions than are other governmental agencies.

The ability of justice agencies to rally to the support of the regime depends on the availability of discretion in the exercise of their authority. If they were constrained by bureaucratic and political forces to adhere to the letter of the law and if the law were sufficiently detailed to prohibit any leeway in its administration, the work of the justice personnel would be purely ministerial; it could as well be programmed into a computer. The personnel could not quickly respond to new challenges in the regime's authority. The previous chapters, however, have shown that the opposite is more nearly the truth: the law provides considerable leeway, and this leeway is expanded by bureaucratic and political power.

Discretion is used to provide flexibility along three separate dimensions. First, it is used to permit city governments to adjust their policing styles to meet what they perceive as their current needs. Thus, they may direct aggressive patrolling against blacks, or they may target drunks; they may direct their attention to juveniles, or they may shift their attention to prostitutes and homosexuals. Particular sets of "outlaws" may be defined and thrown into the justice system. This flexibility, for instance, permits police to target political demonstrators who seem to threaten the regime while leaving other demonstrators—perceived as harmless or even supportive—alone.

Second, discretion permits the justice agencies to suppress particular practices while leaving others (also outlawed in the statute books) alone. Property theft that is considered petty by police is not investigated, and those who report it soon learn that there is no hope for recovering their possessions (at least in part) because the police give it a low priority. Yet such seemingly petty and largely symbolic acts as draft card burning were targeted for police action in the middle 1960's precisely because they appeared to be an effective protest against national foreign policy—not because they involved significant property damage or disrupted the administration of the Selective Service System. Discretion is used to suppress some kinds of gambling whereas other kinds are left alone, to harass some kinds of businesses (e.g., peddlers) while permitting others (like door-to-door salesmen) to flourish. Most importantly, it is used to avoid imposing criminal sanctions on some kinds of activities which are clearly prohibited by law. Thus, housing and building code violations are rarely introduced into the criminal prosecution process and, when they are, the offenders are not arrested; judges routinely consider them so trivial that they assess small fines when the violators are found guilty. Likewise, pollution offenses are rarely treated as seriously as are assaults leading to bodily harm, although the pollution from one smokestack may injure many more persons than any single psychopath can. However, landlords and industrial polluters are not ordinarily perceived as criminals—they are seen as taxpayers, employers, and contributors to the economy of the city. They usually have sufficient political influence to avoid prosecution.

Third, discretion occurs frequently in processing civil cases; it involves choosing between sanctions to legitimize. As we have seen, most civil cases are settled out of court, and the justice agencies often do little more than legitimize the private settlement. Again the law provides them considerable leeway, especially as much of the law depends on judicial interpretation. For instance, the courts may accept or reject certain kinds of divorce settlements; they may agree to legitimize rent withholding or may reject it as an acceptable form of pressure on delinquent landlords. In the 1960's, they had almost complete freedom to order cross-town school bussing to promote desegregation of public schools. Thus, the justice agencies may determine access to the courts by regulating the remedies made available to litigants.

Another characteristic of the justice system has equally important results; it is the fragmentation of functions and powers in the justice system. We have observed in the previous chapters that power is divided between prosecutor, defense counsel, and judges; between private lawyers and public officials; and between agents of one level of government (e.g., city or county) and agents of other levels (e.g., the national government). Such fragmentation has multiple consequences. Although we speak of a "justice system," it is an uncoordinated set of agents. They often work cooperatively because they perceive common interests, but they are not directed by common instructions. Although prosecutors and judges usually collaborate, they also sometimes feud, each charging the other with obstructing what they consider to be the path of true justice. Thus, one policy rarely guides the administration of justice in a city; most cities accommodate themselves to multiple policies.

These multiple policies also reflect differential access by interest groups to the several independent justice agencies operating in the city. One set may be controlled by the local governing coalition and operates according to its guidelines. Another set, however, is responsive to the state or national governing coalition, and one of the goals of this state or national coalition may be to embarrass the local authorities. Hence, they may order a narcotics raid or a gambling raid without informing local law enforcement authorities; they may investigate local officials in the hope of charging them with income tax evasion or mail fraud; they may aid locally oppressed groups by harassing the police with indictments while the police torment the local groups with arrest.

As in the other political arenas in the United States, fragmentation in the justice agencies creates some confusion, some apparent inefficiency, and the opportunity for groups and individuals to choose the most hospitable set of officials to process their claims. Such an array of potentially agreeable authorities is most advantageous to litigants with considerable financial resources; the poor cannot shop for the "right" police agency, judge, or court because they lack both the informational and the financial resources necessary for such a search.

Fragmentation is probably associated with the size of the urban community. Small towns weave a tighter net around their residents; local institutions in small towns are more likely to be controlled by a single elite which enjoys widespread support in the community. Large cities are governed by many overlapping elites, each of which represents only a segment of the total community. For the administration of justice, the higher degree of fragmentation in larger cities means that more opportunities exist in large cities for competing groups to use the legal system for their own ends, that apparent inequities flourish—such as disparities in sentences given to convicted criminals in different parts of the same city—and that large cities cannot harness the legal system to mount a coordinated assault on any social problem.

INDEX

141